MY EUPHORIC QUILL

ALENA SARA THOMAS

For my dear loved ones,

You are the reason I write, the inspiration behind every word and every
lesson shared.

Contents

Contents

Contents

Contents

Preface

"My Euphoric Quill" is a heartfelt collection of prose and poetry that explores the many aspects of life, including its joys, struggles, lessons, and personal growth. Each piece in this book celebrates the value of small, everyday moments that we often overlook but that truly matter. These pages reflect my journey of accepting both the highs and lows of life, finding happiness in simple things, and learning to grow from every experience.

The prose shares personal reflections and stories, highlighting moments of strength, hope, and gratitude. The poetry expresses deep emotions, turning them into words that speak directly to the heart. Together, they tell a story of self-discovery, showing the beauty of life, even in its imperfections.

This book is a small part of my life, shared in the hope that it inspires you to appreciate the present moment. It encourages us to grow through challenges, celebrate our progress, and find joy in the small things that make life meaningful.

I hope these pages offer comfort during difficult times, warmth when you feel uncertain, and encouragement as you move forward on your own path. May this book remind you that even the simplest moments can be full of meaning and that every step you take is worth celebrating.

With Gratitude, Alena.

Acknowledgements

First and foremost, I would like to thank the almighty for being my constant source of strength, wisdom and guidance. Without His grace none of this would have been possible.

To Dr. Samuel Rufus, Thank you for your invaluable guidance and encouragement throughout this journey. Your belief in my abilities and your insights helped shape this book into what it is today.

To Megha Sumesh, your patient proofreading and support mean the world to me. Thank you for lending your time and effort to ensure this book became its best version.

To Angel Mariam Thomas, Thank you for bringing my vision to life through your beautiful cover design. I am grateful to you for making this book visually pleasing.

To my Dad, Mom and Brother, your love and support have been my foundation. Thank you for standing by me, cheering me on, and reminding me of my purpose when I needed it the most.

To my grandfather, Thank you for the hidden contribution you have been offering throughout this journey. Your encouragement has been an inspiring force for me to move forward.

To my best friends, you've been my true encouragement and my biggest cheerleaders. Thank you for believing in me, lifting me up, and being a constant source of motivation.

PROSE

1. Embracing Self Awareness.

I am Alena. I am a normal girl with ordinary talents. If I introduce myself this way, what makes me different? What makes me unique?

Most people, including myself, often become insecure and shy away from life's challenges because they lack self-awareness about their potential.

Self-awareness plays a major role in the personal growth and well-being of an individual. It involves understanding and keeping track of your strengths and weaknesses. Interestingly, our strengths can sometimes turn into weaknesses, and what we once considered a weakness may later become a strength.

For instance, in school, I had a hard time making friends, and I saw it as a flaw. However, in college, I don't see this as an issue anymore; in fact, it has turned into a strength.

I remember starting a personal diary to jot down my emotions, but instead of writing what I truly felt, I wrote as though someone else might read it. That's not the way to write a diary. You need to be honest and authentic in that personal space. Set strong boundaries to protect your privacy, and don't shy away from being yourself.

Confidence is essential, but overconfidence can be detrimental. When someone gives you advice, take it and reflect on it instead of blindly trusting yourself. They might be wrong, or you might realize there's something you need to change.

Now, I can confidently say, I am Alena Sara Thomas. I am a talented person with a beautiful personality. Do you see the difference?

To conclude, life is full of challenges, and you are the pilot of your own plane. So, fly high and safely, with a clear understanding of your surroundings. Embrace yourself and stay self-aware.

2. Pain Behind Every Smile.

For those who think life is unfair:

"The prettiest smiles hide the deepest secrets. The prettiest eyes have cried the most tears, and the kindest hearts have felt the most pain." – A beautiful soul.

Behind every smile lies a hidden story.

I once had a teacher who radiated positivity. She always wore a beautiful smile on her face and loved teaching her students, putting her maximum effort into everything she did. Seeing her so positive, I assumed she didn't face many trials in life and wished I could be like her. But was that the reality? No.

One day, we had a personal conversation with her and discovered how melancholic her life truly was. She narrated an incident where she was on the verge of losing her life and spoke about the daily struggles she faced—things we couldn't have imagined. She hid all her pain behind a smile.

I still remember jokingly asking her, "Should I write a book about your life? There's so much material for the plot." She laughed and replied, "You only know two percent of my life." That one line struck me deeply. Her smile wasn't just a sign of happiness—it was a mask for her fears and troubles.

Just like her, every single person on Earth faces countless problems in their lives, whether or not they choose to express them openly. The next time you find yourself wishing to be someone else, remember that everyone's life has its share of unseen struggles, hidden from the world outside their private bubble.

Remember, you are a beautiful human being who deserves to smile, openly and honestly while facing your fears and trials. Smiles are often used as a shield against the harsh realities of life. Instead of letting your smile become a mask that hides the truth, use it to bring happiness to yourself and those around you.

Behind every smile is a symbol of courage and hope. A true smile can light up even the darkest paths.

Keep smiling genuinely and accept life as it is.

3. Little Things Matter.

"Sometimes it's the little things that make life worth living." – Nadine Gordimer

Noticing and appreciating the little things around you can make a huge difference in your life. People often say, "The bigger, the better," but that's not always true. Sometimes, it's the small details that bring a unique kind of joy—one that big achievements might never offer. A hot cup of coffee made by your mom, a smile from a stranger, or a compliment from a loved one—simple moments like these can make your heart truly happy. When someone listens to you with genuine interest or notices you're not feeling well just by looking at you, you feel loved and cared for.

Imagine a day like this:

You wake up and start the day with a smile. You drink a hot cup of coffee and thank your mom for making it. You enjoy a delicious breakfast. On your way out, your auto driver says, "Thank you." You get on the bus and find a seat while others are left standing. You offer your seat to an elderly lady, and she smiles at you warmly. You arrive at college, and your professors greet you with smiles. During your day, you take a walk around the campus and notice the beauty of flowers, trees, butterflies, deer, and even peacocks (this applies only to MCC students, I believe). Feeling inspired, you write a poem admiring nature. And the day continues with moments like these.

Isn't this the kind of day we all hope for? While you can't expect everyone to be nice to you or for everything to go according to plan, you can be nice to others and make someone's day a little brighter.

Try giving someone a genuine compliment, offering help when they need it, sharing small handmade gifts, cracking jokes, or expressing your gratitude—all while respecting their space. Noticing little things like these will undoubtedly make us feel happier and more content.

Paying attention to the tiny details also helps us understand that life is not just about achieving big goals but also about enjoying the journey along the way. To reach great heights, we need to value the small moments that bring happiness and fulfillment.

I remember my mom teaching me that a one-rupee coin should be respected just as much as a hundred-rupee note because, without the one, the hundred cannot be made. In the same way, the little things matter, they build the foundation for the bigger things in life.

So, take a moment to notice and cherish the small joys.

4. Misunderstanding.

"Misunderstandings are the inevitable wounds of imperfect communication." – Bryan McGill

The greatest misunderstandings in life arise when we fail to communicate clearly and expect others to read our minds. I have often been misunderstood, not because of how others interpreted my words, but due to my own mistakes in phrasing things. Just yesterday, I made a statement that was misinterpreted. Instead of correcting it and clarifying what I actually meant, I chose to go along with it, unwilling to admit my error. Such small misunderstandings can influence how people perceive you and may even diminish their respect for you.

When college began, I expected everyone to understand me without needing to express myself clearly, just as my school friends always did. I now realize that there is nothing wrong with admitting when I am wrong. I've always had a good reputation, and I naïvely assumed people would interpret my words positively. Instead of taking their feedback constructively, I often overthink and spend the rest of the day questioning myself. Additionally, I fear being spoken of poorly behind my back, a likely outcome if I fail to accept and admit my mistakes.

I have come to understand how misunderstandings can damage beautiful friendships or any relationship, for that matter. The lesson I've learned is to own up to my mistakes and not expect others to perfectly understand my words without effort on my part. I am deeply grateful to my friends who have taught me this lesson, especially the one who said, "If you say she killed someone, I can only take it that way. I can't interpret it differently." That remark made me reflect on and recognize my mistake.

It's important to think from others' perspectives and admit your mistakes without embarrassment, even when it's difficult. Misunderstandings are inevitable, but correcting them is entirely within your control.

5. The Art of Perfectionism.

"Perfectionism is the enemy of progress." – Winston S. Churchill

Perfectionism is the pursuit of excellence and flawlessness in any task. Personally, I have been a perfectionist ever since I was a child. I always strive to make everything around me perfect. When I write an assignment or draw a picture, even the tiniest mistakes affect me, compelling me to redo it. I considered this habit a motivation to set high standards for myself. However, as time passed, I realized this was not entirely true. Instead of moving on from mistakes and making progress, I would remain stuck, correcting them repeatedly until they were perfect. This mindset put immense pressure on me and started destroying the joy I once found in progressing.

Now, I do my tasks correctly and on time, but I have also started accepting that not everything in life can be perfect or flawless. The same applies to people around you—nobody is perfect.

At some point in their lives, everyone tries too hard to perfect themselves, feeling dissatisfied with who they are or what they do. It's crucial to understand that life is much more than that. Sacrificing your happiness in pursuit of flawlessness is simply not worth it. Humans are not meant to be perfect—that's a fact and a reality we must accept.

This doesn't mean you shouldn't be dedicated. Dedication is essential to succeed in life. You must put in your best effort for every task you undertake. However, you shouldn't push yourself to perfection beyond reason, as it may lead to chaos and burnout. Your happiness is in your hands, so cherish and protect it.

When used wisely, perfectionism can be a blessing. If misused, it becomes a curse. Strive not to be a perfectionist but a dedicated and content human being.

6. The Jar of Blessings.

What seems to us bitter trials are often blessings in disguise"- Oscar Wilde.

Today, while I was in church, I heard the Sunday school children singing, "Count your blessings, name them one by one, and it will surprise you what the Lord has done." This beautiful song captures the essence of what I want to share today.

Instead of focusing on our problems, we should start counting our blessings. Often, the challenges we face turn out to be blessings in disguise. At first, I didn't realize it, but getting into MCC was one of those blessings. It wasn't part of my plan, and at the time, it felt like a setback. But now, I see it differently. Sometimes, the things that seem like our greatest problems can become our biggest blessings.

To truly embrace this mindset, we should start a simple practice: write down one thing we are grateful for, or one blessing we recognize, every day and place it in a jar. Then, at the end of the year, we can read through all of these notes and see just how blessed we are. It might surprise us to realize how much goodness surrounds us, goodness we were once blind to.

Life is full of unexpected gifts, and sometimes we just need a gentle reminder to see them for what they are. So, let's make a conscious effort to shift our perspective, to find joy in the small things, and to trust that even our struggles have a purpose. After all, when we start counting our blessings, we often find they were always there, just waiting to be seen.

7. Living In the Moment.

"Yesterday is history, tomorrow is a mystery, today is a gift, which is why we call it the present"- Bil Keane

This quote beautifully captures the idea that the present is indeed a gift, one we often fail to recognize and appreciate. Living in the moment is not just about capturing photographs; it's about rooting these experiences deeply into our core memory. It's about fully embracing every present moment, whether it brings us joy or sorrow, and treasuring it.

I've noticed that the older generation seems to live in the moment more than we do. When they attend a concert or a program, they are less concerned with capturing the perfect photo or video for social media. Instead, they focus on observing everything around them, interacting with others, and truly experiencing the event. They are fully present, engaging all their senses in the experience.

On the other hand, we often get caught up in trying to capture everything. We take countless photos and videos, often with the intention of sharing them online or saving them for later. While there is nothing wrong with wanting to capture a moment, we sometimes become so focused on our screens that we miss the actual moment unfolding before us. We forget to let our eyes, rather than our camera lenses to absorb the colors, the sounds, the emotions, and the energy of the moment. We miss out on creating a lasting memory that we can carry with us.

Living in the moment doesn't mean that we should abandon social media or avoid photographs altogether. It means finding a balance. We can still capture the highlights of a beautiful sunset or the smile of a loved one, but we must also put our devices down, breathe deeply, and allow ourselves to fully experience the moment. We should absorb the laughter, the conversations and the feelings that come with being truly present.

To truly live in the moment, we must be mindful, practice gratitude, and make an effort to be present. It requires us to slow down, to pause, and to let go of the need for constant documentation. It is about recognizing that life is happening right now and that each moment, in its imperfection it is worth living deeply.

By learning to live more in the moment, we not only create richer memories but also lead more meaningful and fulfilled lives.

8. I Trust You!

"To be trusted is a greater compliment than being loved" _George Mac Donald.

Trust is a deeply beautiful word for an emotion that involves two people bound together by a silent agreement to open their hearts and be vulnerable, showing their true selves. We might say "I love you" to every person we are friends with, but saying "I trust you" is something different. It is more divine and bonded by an unseen thread. Trust shows us how to walk in somebody's shoes and be empathetic.

To me, personally, trust is more than just an expression. When you give a piece of yourself to another person, you accept them and believe that they will take care of it without misusing it, which requires a kind of acceptance that is immense. Trust also requires respect. Knowing a person deeply shows their true side; no matter what they are going through, you must be able to respect them and comfort them through their dark times.

Trust is earned over time, through countless memories and honesty. I trust my family and a few of my friends, which makes me open up about my fears, my imperfections, or my dreams to them without being scared of being judged or rejected.

Trust has its own negative side to it. Trusting a person means taking a risk and accepting the possibility of being betrayed. The ones you trust the most today might end up being your biggest enemies tomorrow. Having your personal information will not help the situation but make it worse. We have all been betrayed at least once in life, and that experience teaches us not to trust any person easily. Trust is not blind faith, but a conscious decision to believe in someone.

A person once said, "Trust takes years to build, seconds to break, and forever to repair." Once trust is broken, it is broken. No matter how hard you try to fix it, it can never be what it was before it was broken. When you are in a situation where you fight or have a misunderstanding with someone close, never use their personal information or what they trusted you with against them, no matter what. That shows your personality. No matter what, you should be in a position to keep the information to yourself and not take advantage of it. A broken vase can be fixed, but it cannot be as strong as it was before being broken.

Trust is the foundation of all meaningful relationships that requires both courage and vulnerability. It is through trust that we truly learn to love and be loved. If I say "I trust you" to you. That means you are so precious to me and I will treasure with my whole heart and be there for you through your ups and downs in your life.

9. Is It Too Late?

"No matter how far you have gone on the wrong road, you can always turn around." — Turkish Proverb

It is never too late to change your goals or dreams and move toward a different path, but doing so requires a magical ingredient that is time. I've heard people say it's never too late to start over, but lately, I've been wondering if that's true. Whenever I made a mistake, my mom would tell me, "Don't worry, you have time." I used to believe her — that I could always catch up, always fix things. But now, in college, I'm starting to question if I really do have time.

When I got here, I had this idea of how things would go, I'd figure out my career path, find my people, and get on track towards the perfect future. But it hasn't been like that at all. I've changed my goals multiple times and had days where I felt completely lost. Every time I see my friends who seem to know exactly what they want, I wonder, "Is it too late for me to figure it out?"

I talked about this with a friend, and she said, "You're not behind; you're just figuring out what's right for you." That stuck with me. I realized the problem isn't time; it's my fear of failing, of wasting time on the wrong things, or not calculating everything. I've been so afraid of making the wrong move that I haven't made many moves at all.

So, I've decided to stop asking if it's too late and start asking, "What can I do now?".

I'm trying new things. I'm reaching out to people I admire, signing up for classes outside my comfort zone, and letting myself believe that not having it all figured out is okay.

I'm learning it's less about running out of time and more about being willing to make mistakes and start again. Maybe it's not too late to change directions or discover something new. Maybe I'm just beginning and right now, that feels like more than enough.

I have faith that, in the end, things will turn out well and I will be successful. These small trials in making the right decision can weigh me down, but I won't let them weaken me.

10. My Journey of Cultural Adaptation.

"Belonging is the delicate balance between honoring where you come from and embracing where you are."_ Anonymous.

Growing up as a Malayali girl in Chennai, I constantly felt a difference between my home life and my school life. At home, we watched Malayalam movies and listened to Malayalam songs, but at school, my friends talked about Tamil songs and movies, which I wasn't familiar with. No matter how hard I tried, I never felt fully included in their conversations.

My food was different too, and while everyone loved it because it was unique, it also set me apart. I remember teachers asking about the Kerala rice I brought, which was much larger than theirs. While people often asked me for Onam treats or Kerala special foods, I appreciated the curiosity but there were times when I felt lonely and left out.

I often wished for a Malayali friend who would make me feel included. But after the COVID-19 pandemic, things changed. I started watching Tamil movies, listening to Tamil songs, and gradually began to appreciate Tamil culture and food. I felt more included than ever before.

Now in college, I finally have the Malayali friends I always dreamed of, but it feels different. Having spent so many years trying to fit in with Tamil friends, I now find myself more aligned with them. Adapting again to a new environment and culture is challenging. When my Malayali friends say something negative about Tamilians, I feel offended, forgetting that these were my thoughts as a child before

I knew and accepted them.

It is really hard to adapt to a culture that you are not part of, but it's also a journey of finding where you truly belong. In my experience, I have realized that being open to new cultures has enriched my life, but it has also made me question where my heart truly feels at home. And so, I find myself not truly belonging to one world or the other, but instead, to the beautiful space in between where both cultures meet.

11. The Story of Berry and Honey.

My friend shared this hilarious story with me, and I couldn't stop laughing, so I thought I'd share it with you.

She was strolling down the street, casually glancing at all the stores, hotels, and shopping malls when suddenly, a craving hit her like a lightning bolt — chicken biriyani! Unable to resist, she made a quick run to a nearby biriyani shop. But just as she was about to order, a thought struck her: "Wait a minute, didn't I just have chicken biriyani last week... and the week before that?" She realized that maybe spending more money on yet another plate of biriyani wasn't the most financially responsible choice. "I should really use my money for something more useful," she thought.

So, with the noble intention of saving money, she stepped out of the shop. That's when her eyes landed on a pet adoption center right across the street. And somehow, in a twist of logic that only she could comprehend, she decided, "If I can't have chicken biriyani, I'll just get a chicken!" (Yeah, her love for chicken runs deep.)

But, of course, she didn't stop at just one chick — no, that would be lonely. So, she adopted two! Chick number one and Chick number two, who were already best buddies, came home with her. Her family was surprised, but to her delight, everyone loved the new feathery additions.

Then came the time to name her new pets. She, being the quirky genius she is, decided to name them "Biri" and "Yani" — because, well, that's what she was craving when she got them. But her mom, trying to put some common sense into the situation, suggested something less... food-like.

So, my friend put on her thinking cap and rebranded "Biri" as "Berry" and "Yani" as "Honey."

But, let's be honest — in her heart, they'll always be "Biri" and "Yani," the closest she could get to biriyani without breaking her wallet!

12. The Beauty of Colors.

There is something mesmerizing about colors. They stir the senses, evoke emotions, and bring meaning to everything around us. Colors aren't just visual; they're emotional, personal, and deeply connected with our lives in ways that we often overlook. Each color holds its own story, its own feeling, and its own ability to paint the world in ways words never can.

For me, colors are like silent companions that walk with me through the dark. They define moods, they capture memories, and they express what words sometimes fail to. Think of the deep blue ocean, a color that seems to hold both mystery and peace at the same time. When I stare into that expanse of blue, I'm reminded of the feeling of being small, yet deeply connected to something vast and timeless. It's a color that speaks of both adventure and serenity, a thing that I find endlessly comforting.

And then there's green, the color of life itself. Growing up, I would spend hours staring at the trees swaying in the breeze, amazed at how different shades of green could reflect so many things vibrant and young in the spring, deep and earthy in the summer, and fading as autumn approached. Green always felt like renewal to me, a promise that life moves forward, and that with every ending comes a new beginning.

Yellow, on the other hand, is pure joy. It's the color of sunlight spilling through the windows on a lazy afternoon, warming everything it touches. It reminds me of laughter, of the carefree days when worries seem far away. Yellow is a reminder to look for happiness in the simple things, to appreciate the light in every situation. Whenever I see it, I feel a little lighter, a little more at ease, as if the world has paused just to radiate a bit of brightness my way

But then there's red, the color of passion, empowerment and energy. It's a color that can make my heart race, as if the air itself is charged with electricity. Whether it's the deep red of a sunset or the hue of a flower in bloom, red demands attention. It reminds me of moments of courage. Red is life in its most vibrant form that is bold, unapologetic, and unforgettable.

Yet, not all colors evoke loud emotions. Some, like soft pastels, speak in whispers. The gentle pinks and lavenders are the colors of quiet moments, of reflection and tenderness. They remind me of sunsets, of the gentle transition from day to night when the sky is brushed with soft hues, almost as if the world itself is slowing down to take a breath. In those moments, I find a kind of peace, a reminder that not everything needs to be rushed, that there is beauty in stillness.

The beauty of colors lies not just in their visual appeal but in the way they connect to our lives, our memories, and our emotions. They are a part of us, as much as the air we breathe or the words we speak. They make us feel things without explanation, and they paint the world in ways that nothing else can. Each color, in its own way, reflects life, who we are and what we experience.

Perhaps that's why I'm so drawn to them. In a world that often feels too loud or too overwhelming, colors offer a way to see things differently, to find beauty in both the quiet and the chaos. They remind me that life is not black and white, but a brilliant spectrum of experiences, each one as unique and important as the last. Colors bring the world to life, and in doing so, they bring us closer to understanding ourselves.

13. Marks Are Just Numbers.

."Don't let a bad grade define your intelligence, let it refine your strategy."-Unknown.

Growing up, I was taught that success was measured in numbers the marks you scored in school, the grades you achieved, the rank you held. It felt like a race, one where I had to constantly keep up, if not outpace others. Each test, every exam became a way to define my worth. The pressure to perform was heavy, not just from teachers and peers, but also from myself. When I was not able to score high marks, I felt like I was failing everybody around me because that is what I was taught in school. Our educational system, at a young age forces students to focus on gaining marks rather than focusing on what they like or what they are good at.

I remember how a bad grade could ruin my entire mood, and how a good one could momentarily fill me with happiness and pride. But as I moved through school and into college, I started questioning this system. How could a single test, or even a series of them, determine who I was or what I was capable of? The idea that my entire future could be shaped by these numbers felt both overwhelming and unfair. There were times when I gave everything to a subject and still didn't get the marks I thought I deserved. Other times, I coasted through an exam and scored well. It felt random, inconsistent, like chasing a target that kept shifting. And in those moments of disappointment, I learned something important: my marks didn't tell the whole story.

They couldn't measure the hours I spent trying to understand a concept, or the growth I experienced when I finally did. Marks were just one part of a much larger picture. As I let go of the belief that marks defined me, I began to focus on other things on learning for the sake of learning, on pursuing my passions, and on growing as a person. I realized that while marks might open doors but it's what you bring to the table once you're through those doors that really matters. Your kindness, your determination, your ability to connect with others these are the things that define you, not the numbers on a paper.

Looking back, I see that the pressure to achieve good marks shaped me in ways both good and bad. It taught me discipline, but it also taught me that failure is a part of growth. Now, I understand that success isn't just about grades. It's about how you handle challenges, how you adapt, and how you keep moving forward, regardless of the numbers. Learn to learn for knowledge and not for numbers.

14. Nature, Your Teacher.

Nature can teach us the most meaningful, virtuous and beautiful life lessons that no other shall. Nature has always been a silent mentor to me, offering lessons that no textbook or classroom could. Its intricate balance has shaped my understanding of life in ways I never expected. When I reflect on the times, I look outside my window and observe everything around me; the trees, the birds, the flowers and many more. I realize that nature is more than just a backdrop to our existence—it is a teacher, guiding me through its examples.

One of the most profound lessons I've learned from nature is the art of balance. Nature runs on harmony. The sun, rain, wind, and earth work together in perfect way sustain life. The plants don't hoard nutrients, the animals don't take more than they need, and even the seasons know when to retreat and when to show up. Observing this has made me realize the importance of balance in my own life—between work and rest, between ambition and contentment. When I try to rush through life, I remember how even the tallest tree begin as a seed, growing steadily over time without force.

Another thing that I have learned from nature is that, every plant overcomes challenges and try to heal itself no matter what the outcome or result. No matter the setbacks or challenges, nature teaches that healing is always possible, and growth continues, even in adversity.

Patience, too, is a virtue deeply ingrained in nature's rhythm. The steady flow of rivers, the gradual blooming of flowers, and the slow change of seasons remind me that everything has its own time. There have been moments when I've felt impatient with the pace of my own life, wanting things to happen faster or easier. But nature whispers that growth is a process—whether it's a tree reaching for the sky or me trying to achieve my own dreams.

Lastly, nature has taught me humility. Standing before a towering mountain or looking up at the vast night sky, I am reminded of how small I am in the grand scheme of things. This doesn't diminish my worth, but it helps put my struggles into perspective. There's something comforting in knowing that the world is vast, and my problems, no matter how overwhelming they seem, are part of a much bigger picture.

In a way, nature has been a constant companion, gently nudging me to slow down, reflect, and grow. Every walk through a forest, every gaze at a sunset, offers me lessons in balance, patience, and humility. Nature's wisdom is quiet but profound, and for those willing to listen, it becomes a lifelong teacher.

15. The Power of Gentleness.

"Nothing is so strong as gentleness; nothing is so gentle as real strength." -Saint Francis de Sales.

In a world that often equates strength with dominance and assertiveness, gentleness can be misunderstood as a sign of weakness. Yet, as I've grown and experienced more of life, I've come to realize that true strength often lies in the softest of touches, the kindest of words, and the most patient of actions. Gentleness is not about being timid or passive; it's about choosing compassion over aggression, kindness over harshness, even when it's difficult. Being gentle is not as easy as it sounds, it requires a huge amount of patience and self-control.

I realized this when, my friend, who was caught up in trouble due to a false accusation remained calm and peaceful, and explained the situation to the teachers without violence or harsh words, which ended up solving the problem in a gentle way. Her strength came not from overpowering, but from managing the tension of the situation with kindness and understanding.

Gentleness, I've learned, requires self-control and a deep understanding of others. It's easy to lash out in anger or frustration, but to respond with patience, especially in difficult situations, takes far more strength. Whether it's offering a listening ear to a friend in need or holding back a sharp retort during an argument, gentleness builds bridges where harshness often burns them.

In relationships, whether with family, friends, or even strangers, gentleness fosters trust and connection. When we approach others with gentleness, we show that we value their feelings, that we are willing to be vulnerable, and that we seek harmony rather than conflict. It's a quiet but powerful force that invites others to be their true selves, without fear of judgment.

Gentleness also extends to how we treat the world around us. It's in the way we care for the environment, in how we show compassion to animals, and in how we handle life's challenges with grace rather than force. Being gentle with ourselves is equally important – allowing space for self-reflection, healing, and growth, rather than harsh self-criticism.

I've come to appreciate gentleness as a form of resilience. In a fast-paced, often unforgiving world, choosing gentleness is a way of saying that we believe in the power of kindness and that we are strong enough to practice it, even when it's not the easiest path. It reminds me that true strength doesn't always roar; sometimes, it whispers with quiet, steady resolve.

16. Vivid Description.

We were given a small task by our professor, that is to write a vivid description of the person sitting next to us. Let me write mine.

I heard footsteps and looked up to see her walking into the classroom. She wore a blue kurti, her pretty jhumkas perfectly complementing her outfit. Delicate rings adorned both of her hands, adding a touch of grace. Her hair was elegantly styled into a side ponytail which was simple yet beautiful. She smiled and waved at me, her presence instantly lighting up the room. I waved back, feeling the warmth of her easygoing nature wash over me.

She sat down beside me, her eyes wandering as if searching for someone. With effortless grace, she reached into her bag to pull out her phone. What I admire most about her is her carefree spirit. She doesn't follow trends or worry about what others think of her. She takes up all the negativity and somehow makes it all positive, with her presence.

As she smiled at me, cracking a few jokes, I couldn't help but be drawn to her effortless charm. The way she carries herself, so full of life and authenticity, makes it impossible not to be captivated by her presence. There's something about the way she effortlessly owns every room she walks into that leaves me in awe. Even now, as she continues chatting, her laughter fills the air, a reminder of how lucky I am to have her by my side.

17. Self-Control.

Self-control is often viewed as one of the most powerful emotions we possess. It is the ability to understand and steer our thoughts, feelings, emotions, and behaviors in the face of temptation or distraction. It may sound simple when put into words, in practice but self-control is one of the most challenging qualities to develop. Mastering it can have huge effects on both personal and professional aspects of our lives. It allows us to make better decisions, resist distractions, and ultimately achieve our long-term goals.

Growing up, we are constantly reminded of the importance of discipline, whether it's through doing our homework on time, resisting the urge to eat sweets before the main meal or sticking to a fixed budget. These may seem like small acts of control, but each one shapes our ability to control life better with a clear sense of the surrounding. Self-control requires us to look beyond the immediate and focus on the bigger picture, teaching us patience and persistence.

I've learned, especially during my core teenage years, that self-control is not about denying ourselves pleasure or joy, but about finding balance. For instance, the urge to binge watch an entire season of a TV show might feel satisfying in the moment but the regret of ignoring responsibilities for those temporary pleasures, tails along with it. It's in these moments of temptation that self-control tests our willpower, asking us to choose what's best for our future selves rather than our temporary pleasures. One solution to this is issue, finding balance between responsibilities and entertainment and to control ourselves from procrastination.

For me, self-control is closely linked to discipline. One of my personal experiences with self-control was preparing for exams in school. While it was tempting to spend hours on social media or talk to friends, I knew that I had to set boundaries if I wanted to succeed. Every time I resisted distractions, I felt a sense of pride and accomplishment. This helped me build a habit of focusing on what truly mattered and realizing that sacrifice in the short term could lead to my success on a long term.

However, self-control is not just about achieving academic or career success. It plays a critical role in how we manage relationships and our emotional well-being. Our ability to pause and listen in between a heated argument is one example of self-control in a relationship. It is definitely not easy to practice this but it might even save a relationship from being destroyed.

So, let us all try to control ourselves and understand that our little sacrifices of pleasure now can present us beautiful gifts in return later.

18. That Thief Steals Time.

Procrastination is something that most people are intimately familiar with. It's that subtle habit of putting things for the next day or until the very last minute. We often find excuses. It might be saying that we need more time or waiting for the mood to set us right. Procrastination is a battle between what we know we should do and what we actually end up doing. It's easy to justify and often goes unnoticed until deadlines suddenly appears and the pressure is inescapable.

For me, procrastination has been a long-standing companion, especially in my academic life. Whether it's a college assignment or a personal project, I find myself drawn to distractions that promise temporary relief. Scrolling through social media, binge-watching shows, or even indulging in chores suddenly seem far more appealing when there's an important task to be done. The act of delaying often starts innocently, but it quickly spirals into a pattern of stress, self-doubt, and a rush to meet deadlines.

Procrastination often arises from a fear of failure or perfectionism. Sometimes, I find myself avoiding a task simply because I'm afraid of not doing it perfectly. Rather than confronting the challenge, it feels easier to push it aside, telling myself that "I'll be in a better state of mind tomorrow". But, as many procrastinators will attest, that ideal moment never arrives. Instead, it results in a cycle of avoidance, guilt, and anxiety.

The stress from constantly working under pressure takes a toll on mental well-being. I've experienced this firsthand, the panic of realizing I've left too much to do with too little time. It's a feeling that is both frustrating and disheartening because I know that if I had only started earlier, I could have produced something better.

However, recognizing the problem is the first step to overcoming it. I've started to realize that procrastination isn't just about poor time management; it's about addressing hidden emotional and mental blocks. I try to break down tasks into manageable pieces, I'm learning to combat the urge to delay. Additionally, self-compassion plays a huge role. Instead of berating myself for procrastinating, I'm trying to understand the reasons behind it and gradually change my habits. Procrastination may be the thief of time, but it doesn't have to be an obstacle. With awareness and discipline, it's possible to break the cycle and regain control over both time and productivity. Let us try not to let that thief steal more of our precious time.

19. Mom's Marble Cake.

I still remember being distracted by that aroma – the smell of freshly made cake batter. The mixture of vanilla essence and cocoa powder. I used to walk up to my mom and ask if I could help her with mixing the batter. Instead of the electric beater, she would give me a whisk with a small handle. I loved mixing it.

Since she specializes in marble cake, there would always be a bowl of vanilla batter and a bowl of chocolate batter. I remember choosing to mix the chocolate batter so I could sneak in my fingers and lick it. When my mom caught me, I would claim I was just checking the taste.

My mom, being the sweetheart she is, would just smile at me and let me do as I wished. Then came the baking part. Since I loved marble cupcakes, my mom would save a small amount of batter to make a cupcake for me. We would then put the baking dish in the oven. My mom would ask me to study while we waited, but I could only pretend to do so because all I could think about was that delicious marble cake. I also remember running to the kitchen multiple times to check whether the cake was ready.

When it was finally done, the freshly baked cake aroma spread all over the house. We poured chocolate syrup and sprinkled some Gems on top. Then, my brother and dad would join us to eat it. I would also show off my cupcake that my mom made with the remaining batter. I remember this as one of the most beautiful memories with my mom.

20. Virtual Cakes and Candles- 2019.

At 12:00 AM, my birthday officially began. It was October 22nd, 2020, and as I lay in bed, my phone rang. It was a call from my best friends from school. They had planned a surprise Zoom meeting—a virtual party to celebrate! I was both shocked and overjoyed as they unveiled a fun "Who's Who" game that they had created. I couldn't believe they had stayed up late, putting together something so thoughtful. Overwhelmed by their efforts and the flood of birthday wishes, I went to bed with a heart full of gratitude.

The next morning, I woke up to another surprise—a video compilation of birthday wishes. My best friends had reached out to people from different parts of my life, including friends from church and my old schoolmates. I couldn't help but feel so thankful that they had contacted people they didn't even know just to make my day special. Watching that video, I was filled with excitement and deeply touched by the love and effort that went into it.

At 8:30 AM, it was time for online class. As I logged in, my teacher surprised me by wishing me a happy birthday in front of everyone. I was taken aback, my excitement growing with every unexpected gesture. Throughout the day, I continued to receive warm and heartfelt messages from friends and well-wishers. Some were long, filled with memories and love, and others short and sweet, but each one made me feel cherished.

By the evening, my mom had prepared my favorite chocolate cake. As we gathered in the kitchen to cut the cake, the day's events replayed in my mind. Although it was a birthday celebrated amidst a pandemic, it was one of the most memorable and heartwarming birthdays I had ever had. Even with the distance, my friends and family found ways to make me feel closer to them than ever before.

Just so my friends know, I am eternally grateful for the efforts you put in for me.

21. Handwritten Letters.

The most beautiful gift a person can offer is a handwritten letter. It makes you feel loved and cared for in a way that no other gift can. The effort and thought put into every word, the personal touch of the handwriting, and the emotions carried through the ink make it truly special. You only take the time to write a letter when you genuinely love and admire someone, and nothing can replace the joy of receiving such a gift—not even the luxurious presents you've dreamed of.

One of the most treasured gifts I've ever received was a letter from my friend. It wasn't just a few lines scribbled on paper; it was a carefully crafted message that spoke to my heart. Her words were filled with warmth, memories, and love, capturing the essence of our friendship in a way no material gift could. As I read her letter, I felt an overwhelming sense of gratitude and connection. It reminded me of the value of simple, thoughtful gestures and how deeply they can touch us.

Her letter was more than just words on paper—it was a reflection of the bond we share, and every time I look at it, I'm reminded of how fortunate I am to have someone like her in my life. It's these small, heartfelt moments that truly make life beautiful. The letter was beautifully packed with a brown sheet and decorated with red hearts, adding to its charm. Materialistic gifts may bring momentary happiness, but a handmade or handwritten gift from someone you love speaks volumes about the depth of your place in their heart.

I also remember asking my mom why our beautiful tradition of exchanging letters and greeting cards has faded over time, to which she just smiled. My mom has a whole box filled with letters and greeting cards she received from her mother, father, brother, and other relatives. I wish we still had that tradition today—it feels like such a meaningful way to stay connected and show love but let us be happy with what we have today and cherish the present.

22. The Coffee Shop of My Dreams.

I am sitting in a cozy warm cup of nicely made hot chocolate. There is gentle breeze from the open window caressing my cheeks and bringing a red hue to my face. The muffled conversations in the background and soft clinging of tea cups and plates. Despite the sound, it is an extremely calm and serene atmosphere. The sun at its golden hour kisses me with its light and I smile as I watch people around me, all living their lives. There are multiple aesthetic posters, diamond chandeliers and golden bulbs, The book section is filled with novels and pretty poetry books. In the background a hear a soft violin music. The coffee shop becomes a place of inspiration. People around me are engaged in lively conversations, working on creative projects, reading books, or simply lost in thought. Each person has a story, a unique journey, and in this space, their lives intertwine for a brief moment. I imagine myself joining these interactions, exchanging ideas, learning from others, and sharing my own insights. The shop transforms into a hub of creativity, where art, ideas, and culture come alive.

I find myself writing, words flowing effortlessly onto the page. The noise around me fades as I become immersed in the rhythm of my thoughts, exploring new ideas, crafting narratives, or reflecting on the world. The coffee shop becomes a sanctuary, a place where dreams are not just imagined but also nurtured, where the energy of others fuels my own desire to create.

As the day fades into evening, the lights inside grow warmer, and I sip my hot chocolate feeling a sense of quiet fulfillment. It's not just about the cocoa; it's about the atmosphere, the people, and the quiet buzz of possibility that hangs in the air. In this dream, the coffee shop is not just a physical space—it's a space for growth, creativity, and connection.

23. My Love for Stickers.

Little things make me happy, and one of those things is stickers. The love I had for them is indescribable. My first sticker packet was a gift from my mom, and that's where it all began. I've always loved decorating, and being an artistic person, stickers were involved in everything I did. Wherever I went, I made sure to carry a packet of stickers with me to keep myself entertained. Every peel from the sheet filled me with happiness. I would stick them on my notebooks, files, and even on doors. They weren't just images; they were small extensions of my creativity.

Since I loved stickers so much, my friends used to gift me a packet of them with a greeting card every year. Stickers only cost 10 rupees, but to me, they were far more valuable.

As I grew older, my relationship with stickers evolved, but it never faded. In 6th grade, my Hindi teacher conducted surprise tests, and for those who scored 20 out of 20, the reward was a gold star sticker next to the score. I studied so hard just for the chance to earn that gold star sticker, but I often lost marks due to silly mistakes. The thought of earning that sticker pushed me to study even harder, and eventually, I did get it once.

Today, while cleaning my room, I found the box where I used to store all my stickers. Looking through it, I realized that most of the stickers were ones I had saved for later because they were too special to use, but I never did use them. Time flies, and that box of stickers feels like a memory from just yesterday. I'm grateful for everyone who put effort into making and buying me stickers because they brought me so much joy. Looking back, I realize how something as simple as a sticker made me feel happy and content. I only wish to be the same girl I was, whose happiness relied on small things like these.

· 45 ·

24. School Trips and Cupcakes

Whenever there was a school trip, my mom would make a huge box of cupcakes for my whole class. On the morning of the trip, instead of being excited about the trip itself, I would be thrilled about the cupcakes I carried with me. They were usually marble cupcakes, a perfect swirl of vanilla and chocolate, topped with a thick layer of chocolate coating. My excitement wasn't just about eating them, it was about sharing them, the way they seemed to have become a part of my identity on those trips.

All my friends knew that if I came for the trip, the cupcakes would follow. It was almost a tradition. Whenever people thought of me, their minds immediately drifted to marble cupcakes, as if the two of us were inseparable. The rich smell of hot cocoa mixed with vanilla filled the bus as soon as I stepped on, and I could see heads turning toward me, eyes lighting up with anticipation.

The moment I entered, I would always hear a collective cheer, "Alena brought cupcakes! Yayy!" It was the kind of reaction that made me feel special, like I was bringing something to the group that wasn't just food but happiness itself. I would carefully pass the box around, watching my classmates' faces light up as they grabbed their cupcakes, each of them savoring the familiar taste. It wasn't just about satisfying their sweet tooth, these cupcakes were a part of the experience, something that made our trips unique and memorable.

Those moments gave me a sense of belonging. It felt like I wasn't just another student on the bus, I was the one who brought something that everyone looked forward to. The cupcakes became more than just a snack. They became a symbol of connection, of shared joy. My mom's cupcakes turned those school trips into something more, blending her love and care into the memories we created together.

Even now, when I think of those trips, I can almost taste the warm, soft cake and smell the sweet blend of chocolate and vanilla. It was a simple tradition, but one that made me feel like I always carried a piece of home with me, wherever we went.

25. The Love-Hate Relationship.

A love-hate relationship with a sibling is something I've grown to understand deeply with my elder brother. We have a six-year age gap. Our bond has always been a mix of closeness and conflict, affection and annoyance, shared moments of laughter and silly fights. But underneath it all, we have this unspoken connection that holds us together.

Growing up, he was my partner in everything, yet also the cause of many of my frustrations. I remember the petty arguments that would arise out of nowhere like over the TV remote, where we never liked the same programs or cartoons. I also remember our silly fights over who got the bigger piece of noodles or chocolate. We even fought over something as ridiculous as 'who do Dad and Mom love more.' All of these seem very silly now, but back then, it was serious business for us. It often felt like we lived in constant competition. Even when we weren't arguing, there was this underlying tension, like we both knew exactly how to push each other's buttons. He would be the first to annoy me, and I would be the first to annoy him.

Despite the daily bickering, we've always had moments that define the deeper side of our relationship. He's been there for me when it really mattered—whether it was standing up for me when someone said something hurtful or cheering me up when I was down.

One memory stands out to me. I remember going to my tuition class on a rainy day, but as time passed, the weather worsened, and it was no longer safe to walk home. There was water everywhere, and even water snakes. My brother, despite the heavy rain, came to pick me up. Not only that, but he also carried me on his back because I was scared of the snakes and he didn't want me to get wet. Another rainy day, I called him to pick me up from the bus stop. Instead of sharing the umbrella and holding it in the middle, he held it completely over me, not even caring about his own health or need.

There's a strange comfort in knowing that, no matter how much we may drive each other crazy, we have a bond that can't be broken. It's as if the space between us is filled with memories too strong to fade. The little moments of kindness like him bringing me my favorite snack without me asking, or the way we both can't help but laugh at inside jokes remind me that our love for each other runs deeper than the shallow irritations.

Ultimately, I think our love-hate relationship has taught me a lot about patience, forgiveness, and loyalty. It's in these ups and downs that I've come to appreciate the complexities of family, how sometimes, the people who frustrate you the most are the ones who'll stand by you the longest. And as much as we might fight, at the end of the day, I know I wouldn't trade my brother for anything.

(P.S. I would never forgive him for stealing my snacks and pocket money)

26. My Love for Music.

Music has been my biggest companion when I am happy, sad, overwhelmed, or angry. It calms my nerves and makes me forget my stressful moments. From as far back as I can remember, music has been a source of comfort and escape. It has this incredible ability to take me away from the present moment, especially when I feel like the world around me is too much to handle.

During moments of happiness, music amplifies my joy. I love putting on a playlist full of my favorite upbeat songs when I'm feeling carefree. It feels like those melodies lift my mood even higher, turning an ordinary moment into something memorable. Whether it's dancing around in my room or singing along to a catchy chorus, music has this way of elevating my good times. I have an eye for the lyrics as well. I tend to search for up for the meanings of the songs that I listen to if its a language that I don't quite understand.

On the flip side, music has also been my refuge when I'm feeling down. When I'm sad or hurt, I often find myself turning to slower, softer songs. There's something comforting about hearing lyrics that resonate with my feelings, like someone else understands exactly what I'm going through. It's almost like the music is telling me that it's okay to feel, that I'm not alone in my emotions. It helps me process my sadness and reminds me that it's temporary, that better days will come. Some songs make me realize that struggles are just a part of our lives and that I need to move on.

When I'm overwhelmed, which happens often with the pressures of future and career, music is my escape. Whether it's the endless options, internships, courses, to-do lists, assignments, or the weight of balancing everything, music allows me to take a breather. Just a few minutes of listening to a song can clear my mind and help me refocus. It feels like my personal reset button, giving me space to step back, breathe, and regain control.

And then there are times when I'm angry. Music helps me channel that energy. Instead of letting the anger simmer inside, I put on something loud, with intense beats or strong lyrics. It's almost like the music is releasing that tension for me. By the time the song is over, I usually feel calmer, more grounded, and ready to face whatever it was that upset me.

In every emotion, every state of mind, music is there. It's been more than just a hobby or background noise; it's been a tool for me to connect with my emotions and manage the chaos of life. It allows me to experience my feelings fully while also giving me the space to let go of them when I need to.

Over time, I've realized that music is more than just entertainment. It's therapy, a constant companion that helps me navigate the highs and lows of life. Whether I'm feeling ecstatic or lost, music gives me a way to express and understand my emotions, making everything a little easier to handle.

27. How To Make a Person Happy- A Personal Guide.

In a world that often feels rushed and prejudiced, making someone's day better can be a simple yet powerful act of kindness. From my experience, it doesn't take grand gestures to brighten someone's mood. Even small, thoughtful actions can create a huge effect of positivity. Here's a personal guide on how to bring a smile to someone's face, based on what I've learned along the way.

Step 1: Start with a Genuine Smile

It sounds cliché, but the power of a smile is immense. Whether it's greeting a classmate in the morning or smiling at a stranger on the street, this simple act has the ability to set the tone for someone's day. I remember one particularly tough day in college when a friend smiled at me and asked how I was. That small moment of acknowledgment lifted a heavy weight off my chest. A smile can say, "I see you, and you really matter."

Step 2: Listen to hearts

Listening is an underrated act of kindness. In today's world, people are often too busy to listen with full attention, but giving someone your undivided focus is a rare gift. Whether it's a friend sharing a personal struggle or someone just venting about their day, listen without interrupting or offering solutions unless asked. Sometimes, people just want to be heard. I've found that being that person for someone else can make a world of difference in how connected and cared for they feel but it is definitely not easy. I used to be a good listener in my school days but recently, I find myself more of a talker than a listener. It is hard to listen and if you are able to without being distracted, that means you are such a wonderful person.

Step 3: Offer Compliments

Compliments are more than just words; they can be affirmations that boost someone's confidence or brighten their outlook. However, the key is sincerity. A well-timed compliment about someone's kindness, effort, or even their unique sense of style can remind them of their value. People in college really appreciate my dressing style and I get a lot of compliments related to the way I carry myself in them and it boosts me through all my stress and gives me confidence.

Step 4: Be Present

In a world full of distractions, offering your full attention to someone can be an incredible way to make their day better. Put away your phone, turn off notifications, and focus on the person in front of you. It could be during a conversation or even while spending time together. I've noticed that when people are fully present with me, I feel more valued and appreciated. It's a reminder that presence, more than words, can be a profound way of showing care.

Step 5: Do Something Thoughtful

Small, unexpected acts of kindness can leave a lasting impression. It doesn't have to be elaborate. It could be picking up coffee for a friend who's had a rough week, sending a heartfelt message, or helping someone with a task they're struggling with. A couple of weeks ago, My best friends offered to visit my home to take care of me, since I was sick and my parents were away from home. That act of kindness made me love her more and it also made me feel loved and cared for.

Step 6: Give Space When Needed

Sometimes, making someone's day better means respecting their need for space. Not everyone will want to talk or be around others when they're having a rough time. Understanding when to step back and let them process on their own can be just as helpful as being there for them. It's a subtle but important way of showing that you care about their emotional needs, even if it means giving them some distance.

Step 7: Express Gratitude

We often take people in our lives for granted, assuming they know how much they mean to us. A simple "thank you" or an expression of gratitude can make someone feel appreciated. I've learned that thanking people whether it's for their support, friendship, or even the little things they do, creates a stronger bond and reminds them of their importance in my life.

Step 8: Be Kind to Yourself Too

It's important to remember that we can't pour from an empty cup. To make someone's day better, we need to be in a good place ourselves. Taking care of your own emotional well-being and practicing self-compassion allows you to show up fully for others. On days when I feel overwhelmed, I remind myself to take a step back, recharge, and then approach others with a more positive mindset.

Making someone's day better isn't about grand gestures or extravagant acts. It's about being present, showing genuine care, and taking small actions that come from the heart. Whether through a smile, a listening ear, or a thoughtful gesture, you have the power to create a moment of joy in someone else's life. In the process, you might find that making someone's day better brightens your own as well.

28. Your Genuine Words.

Growing up, I believed in simple things. I thought kindness was just kindness, and laughter was as honest as it sounded. It wasn't until I grew older that I noticed the cracks in this worldview, like faint lines drawn around the faces of people I'd known forever. The reality slowly began to seep in: many of those smiles were polished for display, a lot of kind gestures were just hidden transactions, and words were sometimes just fillers, empty of meaning.

Even recently, I encountered a person getting appreciated and complimented for their work but the same people who complimented them were the ones who talked behind their back criticizing their work. Why can't they just talk to each other

Sometimes, I'd see people helping others, and my heart would lift, thinking there's goodness in the world. But now, I find myself wondering if the help is genuine or just an opportunity to appear generous. The line between the two has become blurred. The way people take to social media to share every charitable act or moment of kindness can feel forced, more like proof than anything else, like they need the world to know how "good" they are. I wonder, if no one were watching, would the kindness still be there?

I remember reading Gabriel Okara's Once Upon a Time, and one line stuck with me: "They laugh with their teeth, while their hearts remain cold." It felt a bit harsh at first, but as I think about it, there's truth in that description. There are so many smiles that don't feel warm; they're polite or expected, like something we wear because it's what we're supposed to do. But beneath those smiles, there's often a distance.

There are days when I think back to my younger self, how she didn't need validation to feel happy or prove her intentions. She found happiness in tiny things like a good song, her mom's homemade cupcakes, or the way the sky looked at sunset. There was no performance, just a kind of honest, quiet joy. It feels like a treasure that I'm trying to reclaim, that I don't want to lose to all these complex expectations and appearances.

In this world, sincerity can sometimes feel like a rare thing, like a little gem hidden beneath layers of polished manners and forced laughs. I hope I can still find ways to be that person who finds joy in the small things, who laughs fully, and helps without a second thought. Maybe that's what it means to hold on to what's real in a world that's become so carefully rehearsed. Let us try to be genuine with everything and set an example for the real kindness.

29. Wishes to my Mom.

My mom means the world to me. She has been my biggest source of support, lifting me up through every trial and cheering me on through every success. She's my safe place, my constant guide, and the heart that grounds me when life gets tough. Every sacrifice she's made and every quiet strength she's shown is a gift that I carry with me, reminding me what it means to be truly loved. Her smile, her warmth, her encouragement are all the treasures that fill my heart and keep me going. She is selfless, talented, calm, genuine and everything one could hope for. In every way that matters, she has it all.

There's no one quite like her, and today I celebrate not just her birthday but every moment of love and care she's poured into my life. My mom is my everything. When I look back on my life, every memory feels woven with her warmth and kindness. She's always been my biggest fan and my unbreakable shield against the world's toughest moments. No matter what I do, to her, it seems like the best thing anyone could do. Her support goes beyond the obvious moments, it's in the countless small ways she's made every struggle lighter, every celebration brighter, and every dream feel possible.

Growing up, my mom wasn't just my mother; she was my comfort zone and my best friend. I remember the nights she stayed up with me, patiently listening to my worries and helping me see that things weren't as big as they seemed. She's cried with me, laughed with me, and shared in all of my emotions. When I felt like the world didn't understand me, she was my interpreter, helping me understand myself when I struggled to find the words. She has a way of making life feel manageable. Even when I feel like I can't take another step, she's there, guiding me. She's the only person who truly knows me better than anyone else in the whole wide world.

She makes the best food, and every dish she prepares becomes my favorite. She experiments with different cuisines just for me, pouring her heart into everything she does. Not only is she an incredible cook, but she's also my personal fashion designer. She has created so many beautiful dresses for me and each one stitched with care and love. My wardrobe is full of pieces that I adore, all thanks to her creativity and dedication.

Though she's a teacher by profession, she's my own fashion designer, and it's something I deeply admire about her. Whenever someone compliments my style, I know the credit truly belongs to her. Her eye for detail and her natural sense of style are what gave me my own sense of fashion.

She never spends on herself, choosing instead to provide everything for me and our family. Her selflessness is beyond words, and I only hope I can someday embody even a fraction of her generosity. I've always felt proud to introduce my mom to my teachers and friends during events, and I am grateful for everything she does for me. In every moment of doubt, she's been my reassurance, telling me that I am capable and that no dream is impossible.

Amma, thank you for your patience, love, care, respect, and selflessness. I remember and cherish every moment with you. Finally, happy birthday to my sweetheart mom!

30. Dear Stranger.

This is an appreciation letter for a stranger who came to my rescue today.

On my way back from college, I had a pack of milkshake with me. I'd bought it two weeks ago, but since I had a cold, I never got around to drinking it. The pack, unfortunately, had a paper cover, which had soaked through over time and suddenly started spilling everywhere, bursting at the seams. My bag got stained, and I was at a loss, with only a few tissues that couldn't contain the leak.

That's when I realized I had an angel sitting right next to me. She must have been in her 50s. Without a second thought, she took out a cover from her bag and handed it to me, helping me manage the milkshake mess. Despite having many things inside her cover, she chose to give the cover to me, selflessly. She even helped me clean the sticky milkshake off my hands, even though I told her she didn't have to.

This beautiful act of kindness from a lovely stranger reminded me that there's still so much goodness in the world. It wasn't just the cover or the help with my bag, she offered a simple moment of care that made me feel truly seen and supported. Sometimes, it's easy to feel alone and overwhelmed, especially on challenging days, but then someone like her crosses your path and shows you that compassion can come from the most unexpected places.

So, To the kind stranger on the bus today: Thank you. Your small gesture meant more to me than you might realize. I'll carry this reminder of kindness forward, hoping to pass it on to someone else in need. We may not even cross paths again but still you offered help when I needed it the most. People like you deserve everything good and pleasant. Thank you so much!

31. A Day to Relax.

We all have busy, tiring days filled with responsibilities and aspirations in life and career. Amidst these packed schedules, it's essential to find out time for self-care. At least once, we need to slow down, look around, and live in the present, instead of constantly looking to the future. Taking even a single day to unwind and find peace can be invaluable in the fast-paced journey of life.

It might not seem possible to pause and reflect, especially when you're on a train that represents the relentless pursuit of work, studies, and career goals. But even as we move forward, we should make time for simple moments of mindfulness. Whether it's setting aside a few minutes each day for activities that bring joy, spending time with loved ones, or just relaxing with music or a hobby, these small breaks can refresh our outlook and add balance to our lives.

After all, life isn't just about reaching the next destination; it's also about enjoying the journey. Embracing these moments of peace amidst our responsibilities can be the key to sustaining a fulfilling and happy life.

32. Milky Bar Lessons.

When I was younger, we had a beautiful tradition that we kept and followed every year during summer vacation. It was like a reunion of cousins at our grandparents' home in Kerala. My brother, two little cousins, and I would meet up and have a lot of fun together. Since we lived in Chennai and they lived in Bangalore, we met only once a year, so we counted down the days until our reunion.

Our bond was strong. We shared immense joy, exchanged tons of gifts, bought each other our favorite treats, and much more. One of those treats was the usual Milky Bar that my mom bought for all four of us. We all loved Milky Bar, especially the puzzle it used to come with, as a carving on the bar. We eagerly awaited the moment when my mom would hand us our Milky Bars.

I had a habit of saving the best for last, savoring every bite of my Milky Bar slowly. When the others had finished theirs, they would all set their sights on getting a share of mine, often managing to convince me with their puppy eyes. I ended up giving them my best pieces, though reluctantly. Feeling upset about it, I went outside and cried. My mom noticed and asked me what was wrong. I tried to hide it, thinking it was silly, but eventually, I told her the truth. She just smiled, and the next day, she secretly bought me a replacement Milky Bar. I was so happy and excited.

Even though I got a whole new bar, it could never quite match the taste of the single piece I got after sharing with them. I realized, "less is tastier." Now that they're in the USA, we don't have those cousin meet-ups anymore, but these small memories we shared will always remain a core part of my heart.

33. Chocolates, Milkshakes And Chips.

My dad loves me a lot, and I think his love language is buying me my favorite treats. Since I was young, whenever I wanted something specific to eat, my dad would make sure I got it. He would bring it home so often that eventually, I'd have enough of it and end up not wanting it anymore.

I had a habit of waking up at 4 o'clock in the morning to study for exams, as I was often too tired to study after a full day of classes at school. Whenever he saw me studying in the early hours, my dad would smile, gently pat my head, and encourage me. Then, when I'd return home after my exams, he would arrange all my favorite treats on my table as a reward for my hard work.

I remember one day when I came home feeling really down because I hadn't done well on an exam. My dad could tell right away that I was disappointed. Without saying a word, he brought me a whole pile of chocolate cookies, the kind he knew I loved. Somehow, his quiet way of being there for me and comforting me, even without words, made me feel a lot better.

Also, since he travelled a lot for training in his previous job, he has brought me gifts from so many international countries.

Reflecting on it now, I realize that his gestures were his way of telling me, "I'm proud of you no matter what." His support and encouragement were always steady, even if I didn't always feel confident in myself. Over the years, his acts of kindness have been like a constant reassurance, a reminder that I'm never alone in facing life's challenges.

Even now, when I see certain treats in stores or smell familiar snacks, I think of those moments with him and feel a wave of comfort. Those treats are more than just food; they're little symbols of his love, patience, and faith in me.

34. Your Beautiful Reflection.

"Your Face Is the Result of Thousands of People Who Loved Each Other". This is a beautiful quote that I came across today and it made me think widely.

The beauty we see when we look in the mirror isn't just about what's on the surface. It's about the generations of love and connection that brought us here. The quote, "Your face is the result of thousands of people who loved each other," reminds us that each of us is a product of those who lived, laughed, and loved before us. Our faces, our personalities, even our quirks and habits, these are all part of the love that existed in the lives of our ancestors.

When we understand this, our sense of beauty becomes deeper. We realize that we're not alone; we're part of a long line of people whose love and hopes flow through us. Each smile or trait we see in ourselves is a link to the past, a little piece of the dreams our family held. We might have a parent's gentle nature or a grandparent's laugh, or we may love music because an ancestor long ago played a similar tune. We're here because of their courage, dreams, and love.

This awareness changes how we see ourselves. Our flaws stop being things we want to hide; instead, they become reminders of our uniqueness. Our lives hold parts of people we may never have known, but who are with us, shaping us. Recognizing this gives us a sense of pride and belonging. We stop chasing an idea of beauty defined by others and learn to embrace our own, knowing it's part of something bigger and more meaningful.

In this way, each of us carry a quiet, beautiful legacy. When we treat ourselves with love and kindness, it's a way of honoring those who came before. Every day, as we live our lives and make our own choices, we continue the story of those who loved us into being. So, when we look in the mirror, let's take a moment to appreciate not just our reflection, but the love that's part of us, and remember: we are beautifully, meaningfully connected to those who came before.

You are molded by generations of love, so when you look in the mirror, see yourself as a beautiful reflection of all who came before you.

35. The Lens of Life.

The concept of a "lens of life" beautifully describes how each of us perceives the world through a unique combination of experiences, beliefs, and emotions, like a camera with an evolving filter. My lens has been tainted by various shades over time, influenced by family bonds, friendships, and the quiet wisdom found in life's simple moments. It's been a journey to recognize these influences and understand how they shape the way I see myself and the world around me.

Growing up, I often felt a bit out of place. I wanted to blend in, to belong, so I adapted to the environment around me. I immersed myself in the culture I found myself in, adding a mix of admiration and yearning for connection. This phase taught me resilience and adaptability, and it introduced me to a newfound appreciation for diversity. With each new experience, my perspective broadened, and I began to see beauty in different ways of life.

College brought another shift in my worldview, as I found myself among people who shared aspects of my background. Oddly, instead of feeling completely at home, I discovered a deeper longing for the familiar rhythms of the people that I grew up with. This phase taught me that identity is more complex than a single set of experiences; it's a tapestry of different influences that shape us. I feel as if I am the odd one out and miss out on the jokes when my friends talk and it has always made me feel bad all along but that is just part of how my lens view it.

It's these little moments, simple yet profound, that I hold close. As I've grown, I've come to realize that happiness is often found in these fleeting details: a shared smile, a favorite song, a quiet afternoon with loved ones. I've made it my goal to reconnect with that version of myself who finds joy in such small wonders.

Now, as I try to live more in the present, I find that my lens has become clearer and more focused on what truly matters. I aim to notice beauty in the mundane, to treasure conversations, music, and nature as lifelong memories in the making. Each day feels like a chance to refine this lens, shaping it with gratitude and curiosity. I've come to see life as a journey of discovering and embracing who I am at each stage, through the unique lens I carry.

36. A Letter to My Future Self.

Dear Alena,

Hope you're doing well. This is your past self-writing to you, with so many things I've wanted to ask and say. I really hope you've found success and are working in a job you genuinely enjoy. I'm pretty sure you've made it there because I know how hard you've always worked, how dedicated you've been to make everyone proud especially Mom and Dad. Keep that strength going; they're rooting for you, always.

I also hope you've settled into a life that feels right, a good home, and maybe even a family of your own. Are you happy? Are you content? Those are the things I care about most.

How is everyone at home? Are you still in touch with friends from school and college? What path did you take for your master's degree? And, just out of curiosity, what's your career like now? (I know—too many questions, but can you blame me?)

If life hasn't gone as planned, that's okay. I hope you're still proud of yourself, no matter where you are or how far you've come. Remember, you don't have to have it all figured out. Just stay true to yourself, keep pushing forward, and know that your past self believes in you.

Take care, and keep that spark alive. I know you'll make the best of every moment. I love you, Alena! <3

37. My Comfort Room.

My last day of school remains etched in my heart as a cherished core memory—the day I truly felt that I had grown up. It marked the end of an era, a poignant realization that I was no longer a schoolgirl.

I remember my best friend and I walking through the campus, savoring every corner, every memory, and every little detail the school held for us. From the vast classrooms to the tiniest moments symbolized by something as simple as a piece of chalk, we admired it all with reverence.

Among all the spaces, one held a special place in my heart—the Communicative English (C.E.) classroom. That room wasn't just a classroom; it was a haven, an emotion. It gave me a sense of peace and comfort I found nowhere else in my school life. Only five students, including myself, took the subject, and that intimacy created a safe space where I could express myself without hesitation.

It was there that I formed a deeper bond with my English teacher, whose warmth and wisdom turned ordinary classes into life lessons. She shared snippets of her life—stories of her triumphs and struggles, that made us admire her even more. That classroom was also where my friendship with my best friend grew stronger. Together, we laughed, learned, and celebrated small joys like birthdays and festivals.

On special occasions, we'd decorate her board with drawings, pouring our creativity into making the day brighter for her. She, in turn, would bring us little treats, gestures of affection that felt like a breath of fresh air amidst the grueling hours of physics and chemistry.

That classroom, with its heartfelt conversations and unfiltered laughter, became my sanctuary—a place where love, care, and friendship thrived. When I think of my school, it's this room and the memories it holds that I treasure the most.

This is the one place my heart still longs for. If I could turn back time to my school days, it would be just to relive those cherished moments in my CE class.

On the last day of school, all I could feel was the aching sadness of losing those precious hours spent in that class.

38. The Greatest Storyteller.

Benches Hold History, They Tell the Untold Stories of Generations Past.

When I sit in St. Thomas's Hall for my class, at Madras Christian College, a peculiar thought crosses my mind—these benches have seen it all. They're not just pieces of furniture holding students; they're silent witnesses to decades, even centuries, of life within these walls.

The weight of history settles around me as I glance at the scuffed wood, the etchings of initials, and the grooves worn smooth by countless hands. How many students, professors, and dreamers have occupied this very seat? What conversations, secrets, and ambitions were shared in its presence?

These benches have been here long before me, long before smartphones, laptops, and the hum of modernity. They were part of an era when ink-stained fingers scribbled on yellowing pages and voices debated philosophies under the echo of colonial influences. They've seen MCC evolve from its beginnings as a modest institution into the vibrant academic hub it is today.

What strikes me most is the thought of the people who once sat where I now sit. Were they nervous, clutching their notes before a big exam? Did they dream of making a difference, oblivious to how their actions would ripple into the future? Did they laugh at silly jokes with friends who would one day become memories?

I wonder about the lessons these benches have witnessed. Not just the formal ones delivered by professors but also the lessons of life filled with heartbreaks, friendships, existential issues, and revelations that come with growing up. These benches hold the weight of more than just human bodies; they hold the emotions, the energy, and the silent whispers of generations.

Sometimes, when I run my fingers over the worn wood, I feel connected to an invisible thread of continuity. It's humbling to realize that I am just one more link in this chain of lives that have passed through MCC's history. The benches remind me that while our time here is fleeting, the spaces we inhabit collect traces of who we are.

So, as I sit here, I like to imagine someone, years from now, sitting in the same spot, having the same realization. Maybe they'll think of me, just as I think of those who came before. And in that way, these benches will continue to hold history—not just the history of MCC, but the history of every individual who ever paused to rest, learn, or dream within its embrace.

39. Talking To the Moon.

I sat on the windowsill, the night wrapping around me like a thick, comforting blanket. The moon, round and glowing, hung low in the sky, watching silently.

"Why do you always look so calm?" I asked, breaking the stillness.

The moon shimmered faintly, as if amused by my question.

"Because I've seen it all," it replied, its voice soft and steady. "Raging storms, quiet dawns, heartbreaks, and laughter. Everything passes, like clouds across my face."

"Do you ever get lonely up there?" I whispered.

The moon paused, its glow dimming ever so slightly.

"Sometimes," it admitted, "but even in solitude, there is beauty. I find solace in the stars and in those who look up at me, seeking comfort."

I sighed, resting my head on my knees. "I wish I could be like you, calm, unbothered by the chaos."

"You can," it said warmly. "Let go of what you can't hold. Be present, as I am every night, and remember: even when I disappear, I'm still here, waiting to light the way again."

I smiled, feeling a quiet peace settle within me. "Thank you," I whispered.

The moon said nothing, but its glow felt brighter, as if to say, always.

40. Kindness sometimes fails.

Kindness is one of the best things we can offer to others. It has the power to make someone's day better or even change their life. But sometimes, being kind doesn't work out the way we hope. It can lead to disappointment, hurt, or even a sense of being taken advantage of. Once, I came across someone who seemed very fragile and in need of help because she didn't have money for bus ticket. Her appearance made me feel sorry for her so I lent her money, believing I was doing the right thing. Later, I found out it was a scam, and they had tricked me. It hurt to realize that my kindness had been used against me.

Another time, a little girl approached me with a keychain and begged me to buy it. She followed me around, and I couldn't ignore her, so I decided to help. But instead of giving me the keychain after I paid, she ran away with the money. I felt cheated and heartbroken, wondering why she had to deceive me when I just wanted to help. The innocence that I had associated with her utterly shattered.

During my travels to college, especially at bus stands, I've faced similar moments. Many people ask for help, sometimes with genuine need, and other times with dishonest intentions. Over time, I've realized that not all pleas for help are true, and not all acts of kindness lead to good outcomes.

These experiences have taught me to be more careful. While I still believe in kindness, I now try to think before I act. It's important to help, but it's also important to make sure that help is going to the right people.

Even when kindness doesn't work out, it still matters. It teaches us to be better, to balance our hearts with our minds, and to keep trying to make the world a kinder place.

I have learned to balance empathy with caution, understanding that while kindness is valuable, it is equally important to ensure it reaches the right hands. These failures, though painful, are lessons in themselves, a reminder that kindness is not about the outcome but the intent behind the act.

In a world where manipulation and deception exist alongside genuine need, it is easy to grow cynical. Yet, I hold on to the belief that kindness, even when it fails, leaves an imprint. It shapes us, refines our understanding, and reminds us of our shared humanity.

After all, kindness is not about being perfect—it is about striving to make the world a little better, even in the face of setbacks.

41. Be The Pot Candle.

As I sat staring at the pinkish-silver potted candle on my desk, the room enveloped in the quiet darkness of a rainy evening, a beautiful and profound thought struck me. We, as individuals, are much like ordinary stick candles—fragile, quick to melt under pressure, and challenging to restore once broken. Life's trials often leave us altered, a little less of who we once were.

But perhaps, what we should aspire to be is like the potted candle. Despite enduring the same trials : the heat, the melting, the restless flicker of life—it retains its essence, both in quality and quantity. The pot around it safeguards its core, preventing it from losing itself entirely, no matter how intense the flame or how prolonged the storm. In this metaphor lies a lesson: life will always test us, but our ability to endure without diminishing who we are defines our true strength. Maybe our "pot" is our inner resilience, our self-awareness, or the support systems we build around us. Whatever it may be, nurturing it can ensure that we don't just survive but remain whole, no matter the circumstances.

So, Be the beautiful potted candle instead of a plain stick candle.

42. Plum Cakes.

Plum Cake: A Sweet nutty Dilemma

When it comes to cakes, plum cake has always been at the bottom of my list. It's not that I despise it, in fact it does carry a unique charm but it's simply not my first choice. My heart skips a beat for moist marble cakes, their delicate swirls of vanilla and chocolate blending into perfection. Yet, every December, when I'm in Kerala, the reality is far from what I crave.

December in Kerala means one thing in the cake world: plum cake. It arrives in abundance, filling homes with the rich aroma of dried fruits soaked in rum, spices, and caramelized sugar. Plum cakes are synonymous with the festive spirit, a dessert staple that evokes nostalgia and tradition. The moment someone walks in with a cake box, I secretly wish for marble cake but prepare myself for the inevitable slice of plum.

Despite my preferences, plum cake has a special place in my heart because of the memories it carries. It reminds me of my grandparents — their warm smiles, gentle laughs, and the joy they found in small moments like cutting a cake during Christmas. My grandfather would always have a piece with his evening tea, savoring it like it was the best dessert in the world. My grandmother, on the other hand, had this way of serving it with so much love that it made even the most reluctant eater take a bite.

Maybe it's that association with my grandparents that makes me reach for a slice, even when my taste buds yearn for something else. It's not just a cake; it's a connection to simpler times, to family traditions, and to the people who made my childhood so warm and magical.

So, while I might still secretly wish for someone to bring me a marble cake, I've learned to appreciate the plum cake for what it truly is: a symbol of love, nostalgia, and the essence of December in Kerala. And perhaps, that makes it sweeter than any marble cake could ever be.

43. Cherry Tomato Memories

When I was around ten years old, a small but delightful surprise found its way into my life. It came in the form of a tomato ketchup bottle, which at first glance seemed ordinary. But this bottle held a little gift—a tomato-shaped lid, adorned in a vibrant red hue and crafted with such charm that it immediately caught my attention.

What made it even more special was the seeds tucked inside the lid. My curiosity was piqued, and I couldn't resist the urge to plant them. At that age, I had no expectations of what might come of it. It was just a fun little project, something to observe and care for.

To my surprise and delight, those seeds sprouted into a tiny, beautiful tomato plant. I nurtured it with all the excitement of a child discovering the wonders of nature. Day by day, I watched it grow, its green leaves unfurling and its stems stretching toward the sun. And then, one magical day, the plant gifted me its first tiny cherry tomatoes.

They were perfect—small, round, and vibrantly red. Plucking them felt like harvesting a treasure I had grown with my own two hands. When I finally tasted them, their flavor was unparalleled—fresh, juicy, and bursting with tangy flavour. There was something uniquely rewarding about eating those homegrown tomatoes, a sense of pride and wonder that has stayed with me but later, for home renovation we had to remove the plant from the garden which ended up giving me a hard time.

Looking back, that little tomato plant taught me more than just the joy of gardening. It taught me patience, care, and the happiness that can sprout from even the smallest of efforts. It was a simple yet profound reminder of how life's tiny surprises can bring us immense joy.

To this day, whenever I see cherry tomatoes, I think of that little plant and the beautiful memory it left behind. It wasn't just about growing a plant; it was about discovering the magic in life's unexpected gifts.

44. My First Kitchen Set.

A vivid memory of my first 'kitchen toy set' lingers in my heart, intertwined with memories of my cousins. My cousins and I used to meet often during vacations in December at my home in Chennai. We would dance together, sing songs, go on rides, play countless games, and eat whatever we craved for. My cousin sister and I exchanged clothes and accessories, enjoying every moment of each other's company.

I remember having a small, cute table adorned with a series of numbers and alphabets. We loved sitting at that table alongside two little chairs for lunch and dinner. My dad would take us to so many beautiful restaurants and ice cream shops, which remain in my heart as cherished and amazing memories. We visited places like the Robot Restaurant, Barbeque Nation, Ibaco, coffee shops, and many more popular spots.

Once, we met in Kerala for their housewarming function. My brother, cousin sister, cousin brother, and I spent time together then. We played a cooking game with the kitchen set that my cousin sister had. It was so vibrant, with colorful little utensils and an adorable kitchen to go along with it. Since I liked it so much, she even offered to give it to me, which was so sacrificial and kind of her. However, it turned out to be a birthday gift from a couple of her well-wishers. My cousin brother then offered to buy me a new one. I hadn't really expected him to actually follow through, but despite it being a busy week, he managed to go to the store and get one for me.

It was a wooden set with steel utensils and a stove. It looked so pretty. When I saw it, I was shocked and loved it, though I couldn't express my feelings properly at that moment. To be honest, the reason I loved my sister's kitchen set was because it was vibrant and colourful, but the one I got, leaned more toward a silver aesthetic, which I wasn't expecting. Still, the effort and love he put into it were indescribably, heartwarming, and that made the cooking set very special. It became my first cooking set, and every time I used it, I remembered them.

I am someone who loves receiving gifts more than anything, and they, as a family, have given me so much, for which I am eternally grateful. I love you both more than you know. ♡

45. The Day I Turned 19.

This has been the best birthday ever, and I couldn't stop smiling! The morning began with the comforting aroma of freshly brewed coffee, made with love by my mom. She surprised me with a beautiful dress that instantly became one of my favorites. My dad followed with a gift box filled with decadent chocolates, and my brother, knowing me too well, handed me my favorite chips, such simple yet thoughtful gestures that filled me with joy.

When I got to college, I was greeted with warm hugs and heartfelt birthday wishes from everyone. Messages poured in, not just from friends at college but also from people I hadn't expected, old schoolmates, friends from church, and even people I hadn't spoken to in a while. Their kindness and love made the day feel even more special, and I couldn't help but feel so blessed to be surrounded by such wonderful people.

One of the highlights was a heartfelt handmade letter from my best friend, Angel. It wasn't just any letter; she had crafted it into a beautiful vintage-style piece, and it even carried the comforting scent of coffee. Her words were filled with so much love, and along with the letter, she gifted me two stunning sets of earrings and a delicate chain along with a brown purse because I recently had mentioned that I wanted a new purse because the one I have is torn. Her attention to my minor complaints is what is shown through this and that makes me extremely happy. I couldn't stop admiring them. My other best friends, Pearlina and Keerthana, surprised me with a gorgeous dress paired with matching earrings, which I instantly adored. They also brought along a pack of Dairy Milk, and their thoughtfulness made my heart swell.

In the afternoon, we headed to Glen's Bakehouse in Anna Nagar, where we indulged in pizzas, cakes, and tarts. It was my treat, and I loved watching them enjoy the food just as much as I did. The laughter, conversations, and shared moments made everything perfect. Catherine, one of my dearest friends, gave me a cute pouch filled with a milkshake and another Dairy Milk, small gestures that meant the world to me. Neha gifted me two beautiful bows, a bow-shaped clip, a pair of gold earrings, and a cute little note. Lavanya's gift was completely unexpected—a pretty box filled with bow-shaped metal earrings, a butterfly bracelet I've always wanted, a lovely card with a sweet message, and some clips. Jessy gave me a glittery claw clip and an aesthetic pair of earrings.

But what truly took me by surprise were the thoughtful gifts from my senior Akka, Sanjana. She went above and beyond, creating a personalized gift that left me speechless. She printed out some of my most cherished pictures and arranged them in a special memory box, capturing moments from my school days, my time at MCC, and beautiful memories with family and friends. She even handmade a pair of earrings for me, along with a cute little box filled with hair clips, bracelets, and other accessories. She also gave me a tiny bottle messager filled with rose aesthetics. Her effort and love were so evident, and it was one of the most thoughtful and beautiful gifts I've ever received. The amount of effort that went into making them is indescribable. There were surprises everywhere.

I cut my favorite birthday chocolate cake after I reached home. We even got Jacob's fried rice and chilli chicken, which are family favorites. As I sit here reflecting on the day, I feel an overwhelming sense of gratitude. From the gifts to the kind words, the love, and the laughter, today was perfect in every possible way. This birthday will forever hold a special place in my heart. Thanks to everyone who made my day special. Shoutout to Libi for immense encouragement all along and all my best friends who could not make it to college today but shared the warmth through the screen and to the wonderful people who shared stories and status for my birthday on Instagram and Whatsapp. Thanks to my friends who sent me long heartwarming messages to me. It all means a lot to me. I will cherish every memory that you all gave me with my whole heart. Thank You!

BEST BIRTHDAY EVER! ☆

46. Jack and Mittu.

Jack and Mittu were my best friends. Jack, a brownish-gold dog with sparkly eyes, lived at my grandparents' home in Kerala. Mittu, on the other hand, was a cute snowy-white cat with a black tail. The memories I have with both of them are etched deeply in my heart.

I fondly recall playing with Jack whenever I visited Kerala. His favorite treat was milk rusk, and I loved feeding it to him. Jack had this special way of comforting me—whenever I felt sad, he would follow me around, nudging me to play, as if to cheer me up. He truly had a heart of gold.

Mittu was part of my life for nearly ten years, and I practically grew up with her. My parents, though not particularly fond of pets, allowed her to stay because my brother and I adored him. Mittu had a calming presence—she would often sit on my lap while I studied, which helped me focus and avoid distractions. She loved milk, and it was always a joy for me to feed her, her favorite treat.

Both Jack and Mittu brought immense happiness into my life in their unique ways. Jack taught me about loyalty and unconditional love, while Mittu showed me the comfort of companionship. Even though they are no longer with me, their memories continue to brighten my days and remind me of the simple joys they brought into my life.

Thank you Jack and Mittu for making my childhood better with your presence.

47. The Beauty of coins.

My uncle once gifted me a coin collection album, where I could gather coins from all around the world. My dad, who traveled extensively to foreign countries for work, became my main source of coins. I would eagerly ask him to bring back coins from every country he visited. Each coin fascinated me with its unique designs, often featuring representative symbols that beautifully captured the essence of the country it belonged to.

Over time, my collection grew, becoming a treasure trove of stories and cultures. Each coin had its own tale, a reminder of a place, its history, and its people. Some coins showcased national emblems like eagles, lions, or flags, while others depicted cultural landmarks, historical figures, or even flora and fauna. Holding those coins felt like holding a piece of the country itself, a tangible connection to lands I'd never seen but dreamed of visiting.

This hobby not only nurtured my curiosity about the world but also deepened my appreciation for the diversity of cultures. My coin album became more than just a collection; it was a bridge to understanding and admiring the beauty of our global heritage.

48. My Golden book of memories

I have a golden book filled with memories from school and family, and it is very close to my heart. That book has brought me more compliments than anyone has ever said to me directly. My friends poured out their feelings about me in it. Everything was so positive that it almost brought me to tears,I felt so loved. Here are a few quotes from the book that I absolutely cherish:

"You will always be my Kookie, Alu, secret keeper, motivator, advisor, bestie, sister, and my other half."

"You are cute, cuter, and the cutest!"

"Thanks for making online classes not so boring."

"You are one of my guardian angels."

"Your smile is beautiful!"

"I have never seen you angry."

"I enjoyed every minute I spent with you."

"I am lucky to have a friend like you."

"There are no negatives to say about you."

"Only after becoming your benchmate did I get to know your kind heart."

"We, Communicative English students, should always stay communicated, even after we all part ways."

"Our groups are incomplete without you."

"Always remember, you will have my support in your life."

"You are so straightforward."

"Thanks for the beautiful memories."

"Once, at Farewell, the red gown you wore took me to Disneyland, You looked very cute and pretty"

"You have a sparkling personality, and we are lucky to be your parents."

"You are an amazing student, You are my own kid."_ My English teacher.

"Where are we gonna go? What are we gonna do? Will we stay together? Will it all come back?"

"For an amazing individual with an innocent soul."

"We are sisters from different mothers."

"It is no doubt that I had an amazing time teaching you." My English teacher.

"My dear Alena, you came to me as a little princess holding the hands of your parents. Today, you have grown into an adult. I am very proud to see you as a good, smart, and obedient student of Vel Tech. Make us proud, Alena, today and always."_ My school principal.

These beautiful words have deeply impacted my life. What a treasure to have! I will cherish this book forever.

49. Why I write?

I write to express my present. In a world where time slips through our fingers, writing brings me to the present. It is my way of capturing the essence of who I am at this very moment, my thoughts, my emotions, and my experiences. Each word I pen is a reflection of my soul, a declaration that I am here, alive, and feeling everything with intensity. I write to show who I am. In a world filled with noise and expectations, writing becomes my voice. It is where I lay bare my vulnerabilities, my dreams, and my truths without fear of judgment. Through words, I reveal the layers of my identity that often remain hidden in conversations. Writing allows me to share my authentic self with the world, unfiltered and unapologetic.

I write to feel the drift, the beautiful, uncharted flow of thoughts and ideas. There's something magical about letting words take their own course, guiding me to places I didn't know existed within me. In those moments, writing becomes more than an act; it becomes an adventure, a journey into the depths of my own consciousness.

And above all, I write to leave a mark. I want my words to live beyond me, to stand as a testament to my existence. I want to store these pieces of myself in history, so that one day, my words will speak for me. They will tell the story of who I was, what I felt, and how I lived. Through writing, I hope to be remembered, not just for the life I lived but for the emotions I share and what I chose to preserve.

Writing, for me, is not just an act of expression. It is my pride. It is how I immortalize the present, honor my identity, and leave behind a part of my soul for the future.

I have not reached there yet but will definitely. One day! One day I will!

50. The Same Me.

If I were offered the opportunity to become someone else, someone flawless, wealthy, or universally admired, I would politely decline. Despite my flaws, imperfections, and the occasional chaos that defines my life, I would still choose to be me. My identity, shaped by unique experiences, relationships, and challenges, is not something I would trade for the world.

I am a mosaic of lessons learned, memories cherished, and dreams nurtured. Every scar, every stumble, and every triumph contributes to the story of who I am today. Without my flaws, I would lose the humility that reminds me to stay grounded. Without my challenges, I would lack the strength to overcome future obstacles. My imperfections are what make me human and relatable, fostering genuine connections with others who are navigating their own struggles.

Gratitude is the anchor that keeps me content with who I am. When I reflect on the blessings in my life, family, friends, and the opportunities I've been given, I realize how rich I truly am. It's easy to focus on what's missing or what could be better, but I've learned that true happiness lies in appreciating what I already have. My gratitude extends not just to the joyful moments but also to the hardships that have taught me resilience, empathy, and self-awareness.

To wish to be someone else is to dismiss the value of my journey. It's tempting to envy others' lives, imagining them as perfect, but appearances rarely tell the full story. Everyone carries their own burdens, hidden from the outside world. By embracing my own life, with all its imperfections, I honor the experiences that have shaped me into the person I am proud to be.

In choosing to remain myself, I reaffirm my belief that perfection is an illusion and that authenticity is the true measure of a fulfilling life. My flaws are not weaknesses but opportunities for growth. My gratitude transforms even the smallest moments into profound joys. If given the choice, I would choose myself every single time, flaws and all, because I am enough.

And in being enough, I find peace.

POETRY

51. Grace in Her Eyes.

I heard the rustling of leaves and the gentle wind,
Soon felt the drops, reaching the shops.
There I saw a girl with a helping heart and a kind smile,
Whose happiness lay in the joy of her customers.
She was thankful for all that she had,
Finding joy in each moment, every little thought.
Her hands moved gently, arranging the wares;
Each had a story, each full of care.
With every greeting, she spread warmth and light,
Turning mundane exchanges into pure delight.
In the rhythm of life, with laughter and chatter,
She recognized the magic in what truly mattered.
A word of kindness, a shared cup of tea,
In these simple moments, she felt truly free.
Through storms and sunshine, her spirit remained,
Holding onto the hope for a better world.
For gratitude was a powerful thread,
Weaving connections that nourished the heart and fed.
So, with each rustle of leaves and the rain's gentle song,
She danced through the day, knowing where she belonged.
In her humble shop, under skies vast and wide,
She cultivated happiness, with love as her guide.
I did not know her; I had never seen her before,
But to me, she was the most graceful girl,
With the prettiest soul ever known to man.

52. The Two Paths.

I stand in front of two roads today,
Not sure which one will lead the way.
One seems safe, the other seems unknown,
I don't know which one to choose.
My mind has me loose.
Reminds me of my chess match,
Every step I took mattered,
The moves were mine to make.
May it be for losing or winning.
My mind says one, my heart says two,
Both paths are there, what should I do?
No guide, no map, no easy clue.
Just trust myself to see it through.
Debates of my mind doesn't help me,
Do I trust the right way? I don't think so.
Each step I take, a new surprise awaits.
With every choice, I learn and learn,
No wrong or right, just ways to grow,
In every turn, a new one will show,
I keep learning and I keep growing.
I choose to rise and repeat, until the very end.

53. Dear Flower.

Through the window came the ray,
Piercing through glass to find its way,
Upon the pot where you would bloom,
Amid the silence of my room.
A fragile bud, so close to wilt,
Yet with some water softly spilt,
You lifted up with graceful power,
And bloomed into a beautiful flower.
Your beauty shone, a sight divine,
More radiant than any kind,
You loved the sun, embraced the rain,
And danced in joy through joy and pain.
You gave to me a gift so pure,
A love that time would not offer,
With every petal, soft and bright,
You filled my heart with endless light.
Now when I see you standing there,
I find a love beyond compare,
For in your bloom, I see the truth,
That love can heal and bring new youth.

54. Glazed with Rain.

I woke up to the pitter-patter of rain,
Welcomed by the fresh petrichor from the lane.
I strolled through my home's familiar doors,
Drawn outside by the gentle downpour.
Admiring the flowers, kissed by dew,
And my pots, now glazed anew,
My mind began to ease, stress floated away,
By nature's balm, this rainy day.
I wandered through puddles, feet bare and light,
Each step a dance in the morning's pretty rays of light.
The clouds whispered secrets as winds softly blew,
And the world seemed refreshed, beginning a new.
With raindrops falling like nature's own composition,
I feel belonged here, where peace feels strong.
In this quiet moment, with skies over my mind,
I realised my calm and my troubles, lastly has passed.

55. My Love, The Moon.

I starred deep into your glorious aura,
You shined brighter than any other creation,
Have you ever lied to me, my dearest?
You did, right? You definitely did.
Last week you didn't even whisper a word,
hiding behind your veil of shadows.
I waited, longing for your light to touch my face,
But you left me in darkness with nothing around.
You say you are constant,
But you change, don't you?
Last week you were gone
The week before, you were nowhere to be seen,
Will you disappear again?
Fading from my sight when I need you the most.
Yet even in your absence,
I still search for you in the night sky,
Hoping to catch a glimpse of your silver glow.
For despite your fleeting nature,
I can't help but love you more with each phase.
You return, always, with promises untold,
For your beauty, my love, the moon,
Is enough to make me believe again.

56. The Richest Scent.

That scent,
Yes, that scent which is powerful,
From the yellow papers of the dusty shelves,
That scent reminds me of my purpose,
The path I chose to move through,
It is a fragrance that roots me deep,
That makes me,' A better me.'
It evokes knowledge and pleasure,
Bittersweet pain and sorrow too.
Stories are made, tales are reborn,
Histories remembered, morals reminded.
The ink and paper intertwined,
Each page stitched with utmost care,
Bound with craftsman's grace,
Where time and memories interlace.
Lost in scent, I remind myself that,
It is the most beautiful scent to ever exist.
This richest scent to me, truely is
"bibliosmia".

57. Those Colour Pencils.

In that box, lie those beautiful colors,
My memories stored in each hue.
A rainbow compressed in wood,
Dreaming of the day it can be free again.
All I needed was that one box,
Cause it always brought me joy.
Those colors painted my emotions,
Revealing to me the essence of creativity.
To sketch, to trace, to shade,
From rough ends to fine points,
They touched my paper with each stroke,
Leaving behind art and a thoughtful mind.
These wooden sticks recorded my imperfections,
Guided my hand, helped me grow.
Each color held a story,
A glimpse of who I once was.
Some are too small for my hands now,
Remnants of a time I've outgrown,
Whether fully or partially,
They still remain a part of me.
No matter what,
Those color pencils brought a happiness,
Nothing else could ever match.

58. The Art of Eye Contact.

Can one glance give you relief?
Can one smile show you happiness?
When two pairs of eyes lock,
Two worlds collide, and time stops.
It brings a euphoric spark,
A thousand stories held in those lights.
No need for words, no need for gestures,
Truths are shared just from that sight.
It's a dance of courage and fear,
To truly look at the one who is loved.
A blink of a second, an endless stay,
In that gaze, night turns to day.
In the art of seeing and being seen,
when eyes finally meet,
There comes relief, washing over you,
To finally see the person,
For whom you have been waiting.
The universe interlaces with eyes,
Hearts rejoice with love.

59. Tiaras And Angel Wings.

In the corner, dusted yet bright,

Lies a pair of wings, feathered white,

Once worn with joy, pure and free,

In skits of grace and memory.

A tiara perched on tangled hair,

Glittering bright despite its age.

Angel wings, soft and light,

Carried dreams that took flight.

Church bells rang, voices soared,

In those wings, a heart adored.

I danced, I played, with a crown unseen,

In the eyes of God, I was an angel.

Now, they rest, aged but dear,

Whispering stories, I still hear.

Of innocence, laughter, and things,

Of tiaras and angel wings.

My angel wings will always be dear,

To the child inside me who misses the past.

60. Those Candies from Mom.

Wrapped in colors, bright and sweet,
As warm as mother's love can be,
A little gift, a hidden treat,
In her soft hands, she brought me three.
It wasn't just a candy there,
Not just a bite of sugar fair
It held a piece of love and care,
Wrapped in paper, folded rare.
A memory of her smile so bright
In every taste, I find her light.
The candy melts, but still it stays,
With all the joy her giving plays.
A simple thing, a fleeting bliss,
But to me, it meant all this.
I still recall that taste so true,
The candy that she always knew,
She brought to me when days were long,
After teaching, tired, but strong.
Even then, she thought of me,
With that sweet gift in hand so free.

61. Portraits of Life.

In every face, a story emerges,

Eyes carrying the weight of their untold life.

It captures more than a just the scene,

The story behind everything we don't see.

A child's laugh spills into the air,

A mother's hand brushes the hair.

Love gathers quietly beneath the surface,

And the lines on the skin are maps of memory.

Now I paint mine, Life paints with no order,

Layering the joy and struggle,

Some strokes are hesitant, some bold,

Each one adding depth to the ever-shifting canvas.

In love, in loss, in moments of stillness,

We lay down the colors of our existence.

Every breath, every pause,

Adds to the portrait, always incomplete.

The walls of time hold these images,

Of days lived, of dreams that rose and fell.

In the unspoken spaces,

We find the essence of what it means to live.

To live, live more the portraits vision.

62. The Talk of Music.

A note begins, like a quiet sigh,
It wraps around you, soaring high.
A rhythm rises, sure and clear,
A pulse like footsteps drawing near.
Each sound a touch, both soft and true,
It knows the things inside of you.
No need for words, no need for sight,
In music's arms, you feel the light.
It sings of joy, of tears we've cried,
Of moments lost and love denied.
A human voice in every tone,
Reminding us we're not alone.
In every beat, a life unfolds,
A story shared, a hand to hold.
Through every song, it finds a way
To speak the things we cannot say.
Each chord a world, each beat a breath,
A melody escapes the grip of death
From hands and lips to sky it grows,
Music, the language the spirit knows.
It dances through the quiet night,
In sorrow's tears or joy's delight.
A voice of hope, a bridge of grace,
Uniting hearts in every place.
A whispered hum, a thunder's call,

In music's arms, we find it all.
The pain, the love, the wild unknown—
In every song, we're never alone.

63. Holding Back My Tears.

Shattered pieces of heart, adrift in my mind,
I realize there's an ocean yet to find.
Standing here with but a few small drops,
While the storm in my chest waits, untouched, unlost.
My tears deserve freedom, freedom to fall,
To express, to be free, can they answer the call?
But can they? Can they truly be?
When judgment lingers for all to see?
My eyes stay dry for the world's gaze,
Yet inside, they're wet in a thousand ways.
I lose, I fight, though they never heed,
The tears that beg but I don't set free.
Behind this mask, whispers take form,
Thoughts I bury, safe from the storm.
The uncried tears ache to be known,
Yet fear of weakness keeps me alone.
But with those I trust, in my sacred space,
I cry and share without the chase.
That comfort zone has always been one,
That one person—my mother, my dearest.

64. That Dreamy Gold Medal.

Always good but never the best,

I stand there, after all I could,

Longing for recognition for once,

I hear the cheers, the name that's called,

But it's never mine, though I gave it my all.

I chase the gold, I run miles for it,

But always find myself at second place,

Or even worse, no prize at all,

The medals gleam, they pass me by,

I reach for them, but they slip from my sky.

I'm good, they say, I'm bright, they say,

But never enough to touch the light.

I've learned the rules, I play the game,

Yet no one remembers my quiet name.

I've held the silver, I've felt the bronze,

But the gold is what my heart longs for.

And in the silence, after the fight,

I wonder if I'll ever shine that bright.

How many times can I stand in line,

Watching others claim what I thought was mine?

How many ways can I prove my worth,

Before I break beneath all?

I am the echo, not the sound,

The runner-up, forever bound.

To watch, to wait, to almost be,

What others see so easily.

I can sing but I am never the best singer,

I can dance but I am never the best dancer,

I can paint but I am never the best artist,

I can run, speak, write and do it all,

But I never am the room's best.

But still, I rise, again and again,

To fight a battle I someday hope to win.

For maybe one day, I'll hold the prize,

And see myself through different eyes.

One day that gold medal will be mine,

I will work hard and work for it to come.

65. October Lessons.

October's beginning, a trial so clear
Of learning and growth with every new year.
Of betrayal and new life lessons,
All through my ordinary sight.
The winds of change, they softly sigh,
A reminder to reach, to always try.
But October's more than lessons deep,
It's the month where my memories sleep.
For in this month, you came to be,
A gift of life, wild and free.
My birthday marks the season's heart,
A time of growth, a brand new start.
So as October paints the sky,
I remember, I am the reason why.
Each year you bloom, each year you rise,
Like autumn leaves beneath the skies.
Learning, growing, and shining bright,
October's gift, your guiding light.
A bitter start will not forever be bitter,
As time passed, it does become sweet.
I learn to grow every October,
Also to live and show.

66. The Wishlist.

Oh my dear santa, Oh my dear candles,
Did you receive my wishlist?
All I wished for is a happy memory,
A pocketful of dreams, some wild, some small,
A starlit night, a sunrise call.
A moment of peace in a crowded day,
The scent of the earth after skies turn.
A whisper of wind through the rumbling leaves,
Time to slow down, time to just breathe.
A book to get lost in, a song to replay,
A heart that's open, come what may.
Laughter with friends, a love that stays,
A path that's lit, even through haze.
A wish for wonder, a wish for grace,
To find your rhythm, your own sweet pace.
A chance to be bold, to dance, to fall,
To live and to cherish, to feel it all.
For all the wishes, both big and small,
Let life's surprises answer them all.
Is it too much to ask? Tell me please.

67. Frocks Or Jeans.

The grace I've learned, a gentle light,

Shifts my mind from black to white.

Through costumes, we define our way,

Yet it's just fabric at the end of day.

But some will see what isn't there,

A world where judgment fills the air.

You deserve the freedom to choose,

To stand tall, with nothing to lose.

Stitch your story in every thread,

Let colors speak what's left unsaid.

No label shapes the soul you keep,

You are whole, both wide and deep.

Patterns shift, and fabrics stray,

But your spirit soars beyond the fray.

Wear your truth, let courage rise,

You are the canvas, you are the skies.

With every thread, you hold the wand,

To weave and break the lies beyond.

See the person, not their guise,

For clothes can never mask the wise.

Be who you are, with pride to bear,

Wear what you love, and never despair.

68. All I Want Is to Heal.

I want to heal and return to myself,
But I'm worn out, weighed down by the sickness,
I long for a gentle touch of care,
The kind I've always been given.
But the situation overwhelms the caregivers,
Pulling them in other directions.
All I wish for is for things to ease,
To become less heavy and less intense.
I feel light-headed, dizzy from the medications,
Everything I eat tastes bitter.
I just want to enjoy food again,
And for this fever to finally break.
I pray, and I keep praying.
I want to see my family smile,
For the laughter to return.
But we're all exhausted,
Each of us carrying our own pain.
Hope for better days fills my thoughts.
My birthday is next week,
All I wish for is good health,
And for my family to feel joy once again.

69. The Box of Chocolates.

I found a box, wrapped with grace,

Gold and black, a dream's embrace.

Ribbons weaved in a pretty sight,

Softly glowing in the light.

A sudden call, my father's tone,

"Open it, it is for you!"

I pulled the ribbons, soft and slow

Letting the magic gently flow.

With each layer, A treasure waiting to unfold,

Chocolates gleamed of dark, white, and milk.

I felt like a child again,

A child who gets excited over chocolates.

But in that gift, it wasn't about the sweet,

It was the love that made it complete.

My heart knew well, it wasn't the treat,

But my father's care that made it beat.

Thank you, Dad, for all you do,

For every gift that whispers "you."

70. The Musical Keys.

Fingers move gently over the smooth keys,
Each sound a quiet echo of something once felt.
Black and white, brush against each other,
Like the moments that blend into one another.
I touch the past, let it linger for a while
A quiet melody of joy and loss.
The future is there, just out of reach,
A quiet hum beneath the surface.
My dream of playing it flawlessly,
Occupies my mind endlessly,
As I play, I dream more,
More, more and more.
Life unfolds like a song, sometimes harmonious,
Other times filled with quiet pauses,
But in every note, in every breath,
There is a way forward, a quiet strength.
Each key holds a choice, a path,
And in playing, I know where I belong.

71. That One Trip.

Ages of planning, months of dreams,
Atlast, we set out on our journey.
Bags packed tight, snacks tucked in, speakers loud,
With hearts light and spirits high, we set off to Pondi.
Through laughter that echoed and tears that softened,
We swam through waves of time and feeling,
Pushing forward until we reached the welcoming shore.
We sang with all our souls, our voices soaring free,
Dancing wild, our hands and hearts unbound by worry.
On boats, we found our peace, nestled among friends,
Gliding through thick forests and tranquil waters.
The world around us seemed to blur,
But our joy stayed vivid, pulsing and alive.
We floated with laughter, carried by the river's flow,
Having fun, more fun than words could show.
Breakfast, lunch and dinner we had,
Together with hearty talks,
We ate until our hearts were filled,
Filled with, only but love.

72. My Sleepy Eyes.

My eyes reveal a weary tale,
Of struggles fought and strength grown frail,
Illnesses that wore me thin,
Yet, I bore them with a quiet grin.
For all of this, though strange it seems,
Was meant to be, like distant dreams.
Through every storm, I tried to stand,
A weary heart, but steady hand.
I crave the peace that sleep can bring,
But my restless mind takes wing.
Yet today, the clouds withdrew,
And joy, in me, bloomed anew.
I feel a freshness in my face,
A lightness time cannot erase,
All because my parents' love,
Lifted me like stars above.
So I breathe deep and smile wide,
Grateful for this brighter side.

73. The Coffee Cup.

In my hands, a humble, sturdy friend,
A gentle warmth that seems to mend,
With whispers of mornings soft and slow,
And tales of dawn's gentle, amber glow.
Its rim holds memories, sips of grace,
Moments of pause in a busy chase,
Silent comfort in a crowded room,
A steady light through fleeting gloom.
It's chipped and worn, yet strong it stands,
A testament to gentle hands,
That lift it up, day after day,
As worries melt and fade away.
Oh, coffee mug, with stories deep,
In you, my quiet secrets keep,
A faithful cup, my dawn's embrace,
In every sip, a peaceful place.

74. Bows, Bows and Bows.

A beautiful thick satin cloth,
Embracing itself into a folded hug,
By pushing a string forward,
And pulling the other backwards.
By a gentle force of harmless power,
Surely It does take time and effort,
Of Blissful soft tender hands,
To get it to embrace itself.
Wanna be that hand of love?
Wanna be that pillow of knots?
Wanna be a bond maker?
After pulling up it comes,
A pretty figure with equal sides,
Round, pink and shiny it was,
This is what I wear day after day.
A bow of embrace, A bow of love,
A bow of bonding , A bow of beauty.
I graces me with beauty and elegance,
In true harmony with my inner self.

75. Sparkling Lights.

Waking up to bursting sounds,
Walking up to the sighting grounds,
I explore the magic of colors—
Blue, red, and green.
To the left, I see golden sparkles,
To the right, silver ones gleam.
I see it all with my heart filled,
With flames of festivity and joy.
On the terrace I stand,
And realize how beautiful it is
To watch families, laugh together,
To light and crackle in delight.
Today is Diwali,
A festival I don't celebrate,
But one I've loved all my life,
For it marks my day of colors.
Every year I wait and wait,
To hear the cracks and see the lights
Sparkling across the plain dark night sky,
I love this day, and I wait for the next.

76. My Unknown Feelings.

There it is, my unknown feelings,
I don't know what this is.
My heart flutters,
a soft tremor, a quiet ache.
It holds me in the silence,
A presence I can't define.
Neither joy nor sorrow,
but a mixture, a mystery.
It sits somewhere deep,
in a place words cannot touch,
only felt, only known
in the shiver beneath thought.
I reach for it, try to understand,
yet it slips through my grasp,
leaving only traces,
a lingering warmth, a shadowed light.
What is this, I wonder,
this echo of something I cannot see?
A truth waiting to reveal itself,
or just a feeling meant to be?
Neither joy nor sorrow,
but something in between,
a quiet presence,
an unmarked territory of the heart.
It feels like warmth and weight all at once,

a gentle pressing, a distant echo.
A place where thoughts drift, unformed,
where dreams live and yet to be.

77. Little Duties.

In small, sweet tasks each day we find,
The simple joys that ease the mind.
A made bed, dishes put away,
A quiet start to greet the day.
A gentle touch, a thoughtful deed,
These little acts fulfill a need.
Though often small, they fill the heart,
In quiet ways, they play their part.
So let us cherish what seems small,
In little duties, life stands tall.
For in these moments, we can se
A world of calm and harmony.
Butterflies, flowers, and birds in the trees,
Each one's busy with gentle ease.
A flutter, a bloom, a song that they sing,
Quietly doing their part for spring.
The sun casts warmth, the breeze hums low,
With little duties, they help life grow.
So like the flowers and skies of blue,
I'll fill my days with simple truths.
In whispers soft, in humble ways,
Life's beauty shines through small displays.
For even the smallest hands can weave,
A world of wonder when they believe.

78. Cloudy Opinions.

Opinions scatter like leaves in autumn,
Each one shaped by the hand that holds it.
They arrive from different corners,
borne by voices we know, and voices we don't.
Some press against us, sharp as thorns,
insisting on edges we hadn't noticed.
Others settle softly, like quiet rain,
seeping into places we didn't know were dry.
They twist and fold, mirroring fears,
beliefs, hopes, and stories long lived.
They ask to be held, examined, let go—
not all are ours to carry.
So we contemplate which to keep,
and which to release back to the wind,
finding the shape of our own truth
among the countless others that float by.

79. In The Heart of It All.

There's beauty in the weight of ordinary things,
in the clatter of tea cups on a tired morning,
the gentle hum of voices in crowded spaces,
each one a life, a quiet story whispered,
into the wide expanse of a single day.
In the grind of bus wheels against gravel,
And the rhythm of steps on busy sidewalks,
I feel a kind of music,
An unspoken song binding us all,
as we pass, as we pause, as we carry on.
Someone laughs, someone sighs,
a child tugs at their parent's sleeve,
and we move through each other's moments,
our paths crossing briefly like shadows,
leaving traces that linger, unseen.
And maybe life is this—
a thousand small things we barely notice,
the warmth of hands, the pulse of breath,
the silent courage of showing up each day,
to live, to feel, to carry on.
In the heart of it all, there is a quiet resilience,
a delicate strength in the simple act of being,
in meeting each ordinary day
with the fullness of who we are—
imperfect, unfinished, yet wholly alive.

80. Yay! It's Gone.

Have you ever felt this before?
The feeling of pleasant emptiness,
Where everything just feels light,
And the rock in your head is gone.
A quiet calm settles in its place,
As worries drift to some distant shore,
Leaving only a gentle space,
To breathe, to pause, and to explore.
The weight lifts, shadows fade,
Thoughts like feathers, soft and slow.
In this stillness, unafraid,
You find a peace you didn't know.
I savor the lightness, the freedom to soar,
Rising higher than I ever dared.
With hope that no weight returns once more,
No shadowed stone to leave me ensnared.

81. Little Memories.

Little memories we make today,
Are treasures in the most lasting way.
Before we blink, the moments flee,
As life unfolds its mystery.
Then comes regret, a haunting refrain,
For the past we let slip, again and again.
Lost in the noise of future and plans
We missed the life right in our hands.
But today is here, your moment to claim,
Rise, live, and set your heart aflame.
Embrace the beauty, let it stay—
For today's gift in every way.

82. Among The Red Roses.

I step into rooms of laughter and light,
Bright petals of crimson, but I'm the white.
Their voices swirl, like winds through the trees,
Yet none of their words ever reach me with ease.
They speak in tongues I can't seem to know,
Names and stories that fail to show,
Any meaning or warmth to me,
I'm a lone white rose where red should be.
I nod and smile, pretending to hear,
Telling myself I belong here, near,
Yet my thoughts drift to simpler scenes,
To open skies, to quiet dreams.
I'm playing a part in a script I don't know,
Their laughter echoes, but I feel the hollow,
Forced smiles in photographs framed and staged,
A story told, but my soul caged.
How I long to find a circle of kind,
People with warmth and like-minded minds,
Where laughter feels soft, and smiles are real,
Where being myself is all I reveal.
So here I sit with a gentle facade,
A ghost in the room, apart and odd,
Wishing to dance, to laugh, to belong,
In a garden where each flower finds its song.
All I want is to feel included,

And not be the odd one in the bunch.

83. Fragile Glass

I am nothing but fragile glass,
Always on the verge of breaking,
Hating how my tears gather fast,
Spilling with each slight undertaking.
My glass gleams, rich, and clear as crystal,
Yet it's still glass, brittle, finite, frail.
One tremor, one slip, one misplaced whisper,
And I might shatter, my strength grown pale.
I'm the glass that holds a world within,
Reflecting skies, both dark and bright,
I am strong, yet paper-thin,
Balancing shadows and streams of light.
Each line, each flaw a silent story,
Etched by time and fragile grace,
A beauty born from fragility's glory,
In breaking, still finding my place.

84. Weight Of the Expectations.

There is a weight I wear,
Silent, steady, shaped by others' dreams.
It rests on my shoulders,
An invisible cloak, woven from hopes not my own.
Each thread, a whispered should,
Each stitch, a glance that lingers too long.
They tell me to be something more,
something brighter, higher, better.
I take each step carefully,
Measuring my worth by their desires,
Wondering where I end, and they begin.
I walk their path, forgetting my own voice.
But beneath this weight,
A quiet part of me stirs,
Longing for a place to breathe, to grow,
To feel the lightness of choosing my own dreams,
To be something softer, real,
Not held to any mold, not bound by any thread,
Just me, unburdened and whole.

85. Pretty Garden

In the quiet of dawn, they softly bloom,
Brushing the earth with gentle perfume.
Roses blush with secrets untold,
Tulips whisper of love, quiet and bold.
Daisies beam like hearts of gold,
Lavender hums in fields of old.
Lilies bow with elegance rare,
Sunflowers stretch to the golden air.
Jasmine scents the summer night,
Violets blush with soft delight.
Dhalia in the autumn sigh,
While orchids reach for the endless sky.
Each blossom hums a silent song,
A fleeting beauty that won't last long.
Yet in their fragility lies their might,
A testament to life's fleeting light.
Oh, flowers, you teach us to embrace,
The fragile moments, the gentle grace.
To live like petals, vibrant and free,
A bloom today, a cherished memory.

86. Butterfly! Butterfly!

A whisper of colors, soft and bright,
She flutters gently, chasing the light.
Born from stillness, wrapped in a shell,
A quiet miracle, a tale to tell.
Her wings, like petals kissed by dawn,
Painted with hues of dusk and morn.
Each fragile beat, a silent song,
A fleeting beauty, not for long.
Through fields of blooms, she weaves her way,
A dancer of spring in nature's ballet.
No map, no guide, just wind to steer,
She travels far, yet seems so near.
Oh butterfly, a symbol of change,
A life reborn, so vast, so strange.
You teach us softly, as you soar,
That endings lead to something more.

87. Approaching Frost.

Cold breeze caressing my reddish cheek,
All I wish for is to seek,
Seek something in contrast,
Like red is for blue, white is for black.
It is winter, the coldness in the air,
A cup of hot chocolate around the fair,
Freshly baked pies and cookies,
The smell and heat fills up the air.
The crackling fire, a warm embrace,
A gentle calm in this icy space.
Snowflakes dance beneath the light,
Turning the world to a canvas of white.
People's laughter, bells that chime,
An endless joy frozen in time.
With every moment, a memory made,
In the fleeting frost, nothing will fade.
So I wander through this winter's glow,
Grateful for all it chooses to show.
In the contrast, I find my place,
A quiet peace in its cold embrace.

88. Grapes and Grapes

A delightful bunch of purple, black, and green,

Ever so gentle as it always seems,

With jelly heart and outer fragility,

As sweet as any other entity.

Nestled in boxes or laid in a bowl,

Whispering stories to delight the soul.

Each bite a burst, a symphony of taste,

A fleeting joy you'll never waste.

Grapes, the treasure of vine and sun,

In their quiet splendor, they've already won.

Purple as twilight, black as the night,

Green as the fields kissed by light.

Carry them forth to brighten the day,

In every form, they find their way,

A symbol of nature's simplest pleasure,

An earthly gift, a timeless treasure.

89. Pretty Curls

I fought each strand with every stroke,
Dreaming of locks that were smooth and never broke,
Brushed and brushed to make them straight,
Unaware of the beauty innate.
But time whispered truths so kind,
Revealing grace I couldn't find.
Now my curls, wild and free,
Are the truest reflection of me.
I fought each strand with every stroke,
In search of beauty, my spirit broke.
I envied the sleek, the glossy shine,
Yet missed the magic that was mine.
Each curl a story, each twist a form.
In chasing trends, I couldn't see,
Years rolled by and time has changed,
Now I wear my curls with pride.
Curls, I love you!

90. The Realism of Love

Love, a tale both old and new,
A feeling vast, yet interpreted.
We weave it as immortal art,
But does it hold such timeless heart?
It isn't easy, nor always kind,
A test of will, of heart, and mind.
Not grand gestures, nor spreading fire,
But quiet acts that don't expire.
Love cannot fix what's deep inside,
No magic cure for pain we hide.
Two souls must stand, both whole, complete,
For love to grow, for hearts to meet.
It's choice, not just a fleeting flame,
A steady course, not just a game.
When thrill fades into steady streams,
Love builds its strength in shared dreams.
Unrequited, it leaves its ache,
A silent lesson, hearts must take.
For loving's power, raw and real,
Is not in getting, but to feel.
It shifts, it grows, it learns, it bends,
From passion's heat to trust as friends.
Not less, but more, it finds its way,
Through every night and dawning day.
But love requires a heart that's whole,

To give, yet guard, your sacred soul.

For empty cups can't quench the thirst,

Self-love and care must come first.

And though it blooms, it may not stay,

Some loves are meant to fade away.

Yet even in their brief spark,

They leave their light within the dark.

So know, dear heart, love's fragile art,

It's not a race, nor quick to start.

It's magic real, yet bound by ground,

A choice where truth and dreams are found.

91. Wish I Could Do More.

I wish my hands could hold the sun,
To warm the hearts of everyone.
To gather light and let it pour,
A gift of love—I wish for more.
I wish my voice could calm the sea,
And soothe the storms inside of me.
To speak the words, both kind and true,
To heal the wounds, to start anew.
I wish my time could stretch and bend,
To be with those I call a friend.
To mend the bonds that time wore thin,
And keep the love that lies within.
I wish my steps could tread so far,
To touch each soul, a guiding star.
To light the paths for lost and small,
To lift them up—I'd give my all.
I wish my heart could hold the sky,
For dreams that fade and hopes that die.
To piece the fragments, make them whole,
To fill each life, each searching soul.
But here I stand, with just my will,
A tender heart, a longing still.
Though small my deeds, my love is vast,
A quiet wish to make them last.

92. What If?

I hold my words, keep them inside,
Afraid of what you'll cast aside.
A simple "no," a turned-away glance,
Enough to shatter my fragile stance.
But what if I speak, let it all show,
And find there's more than fear to know?
A chance, a smile, a moment shared—
A world beyond the fear I've bared.
So I'll take the leap, despite the sting,
For even rejection is a daring thing.
It means I tried, it means I cared,
And that, alone, leaves nothing compared.

93. December's Entry

The air is cold, the skies are gray,
The sun feels shy, hides half the day.
Leaves are gone, the trees stand tall,
Winter's whisper touches all.
Scarves come out, the breeze feels near,
The month of magic starts right here.
Candles glow, and hearts feel light,
December's charm is pure and bright.
A time to pause, to dream, to see,
The beauty of simplicity.
With every chill, a cozy spark,
December warms the coldest heart.

94. Hearty Cravings.

A soft aroma, a distant call,

The simmering pot, the spice's thrall.

A taste imagined, yet so near,

A craving sharp, insistent, clear.

Golden crusts and melting cheese,

Sweetened air from honeyed breeze.

Steaming bowls of fragrant rice,

Chocolate dark, or sugar twice.

My tongue demands, my mind obeys,

A feast of dreams in endless arrays.

The crack of bread, the sizzle's hum,

A symphony from where flavors come.

But cravings tease, they never stay,

A fleeting joy that slips away.

For every bite, another need,

An endless hunger we must feed.

Yet in this chase, a truth so sweet,

It's not just food, but love we eat.

A shared dessert, a midnight fry,

The moments baked beneath the sky.

95. Chilled Hands and Warm Heart

Holding an umbrella, walking in the rain,
Along the sidewalks of the lane,
Intertwined with love on every side,
Happy to walk, happy to abide.
The raindrops dance, a rhythmic tune,
Beneath the clouds, under the moon.
Each step we take, a story unfolds,
Of whispered dreams and hands to hold.
The world fades out, it's just we two,
A canvas painted in shades of blue.
The rain, a blessing from skies above,
An eternal echo of our love.
Through puddles deep, we laugh, we play,
As the storm becomes our hideaway.
No rush, no worry, no end in sight,
Just hearts alight in the gentle night.

96. Fairy Lights.

Tiny orbs of golden hue,
Draped in dreams, a starlit view.
They flicker soft, they hum a tune,
Dancing secrets to the moon.
Threads of magic strung with care,
Weaving wonder in the air.
A glow so warm, a heart's delight,
They paint the dark with borrowed light.
Each tiny bulb, a story told,
Of whispered wishes, young and old.
Of laughter shared, and tears that dried,
Beneath their watch, where hope resides.
In stillness, they illuminate,
The corners time dares contemplate.
A simple string, yet so profound,
Binding hearts where love is found.
Oh, fairy lights, you softly sing,
Of fleeting moments, joy you bring.
You cast a spell, and we abide,
In your embrace, the world feels wide.

97. The Chime of Pleasant Red.

In the chime of pleasant red,
where sunsets softly tread,
a melody hums through the air,
painting whispers, vivid and rare.
Crimson waves on autumn leaves,
dance to the rhythm the wind weaves.
A scarlet thread through twilight's seam,
a tender glow, a velvet dream.
Ruby moments in fleeting skies,
where every shade of scarlet lies,
the warmth of dusk, a silent hymn,
a fleeting fire on the horizon's rim.
Oh, chime of red, your gentle spell,
tells the stories the heart can't quell.
In your embrace, the world feels whole,
a vivid hue for a weary soul.

98. Pulse

Deep within, it beats, unrelenting,
a rhythm neither asked for nor controlled.
It carries the weight of longing,
the ache of loss,
the fierce swell of joy
that almost splits it in two.
It does not pause for breath,
even when you wish it would.
It does not ask for permission,
even when you beg it to stop.
It remembers everything—
every whispered hope,
every scream that tore through silence,
every touch that left a bruise or a balm.
It breaks and rebuilds,
shatters and mends,
over and over,
a cycle of surrender and survival.
There is no peace in its existence,
only the endless tension
between life and silence,
a war fought in crimson tides.
And yet, even when it falters,
it is relentless.
Not because it must,

but because it chooses to.

99. Villain.

Scared, am I? Yes, I definitely am,
Scared of becoming the villain of my own story.
That dark tale of me and those I love,
Where nothing is about I, me, or myself.
Am I merely the side character?
A side character in my own life?
I write the lines for the protagonist within,
But they twist, and the villain begins to appear.
I am what I am. I am who I am.
Can I ever change the script?
A script that looks different to every eye—
To some, I'm the hero; to others, I'm the villain.
Okay, but not okay—who can explain it?
That feeling of being the villain in my own tale?
There's only one answer. Just one.
Be kind, be empathetic, be your better self.

100. Oh My, Oh My Love!

Oh, my love! Oh, my love!
In the quiet cadence of the moon's glow,
You are the echo within my veins,
A whisper in the forgotten corners of time,
A symphony of stars, only I can know.
Oh, my love! Oh, my love!
Beneath the veils of the restless sky,
Your presence lingers like an ancient dream,
Carved in the stone of forgotten realms,
Where shadows and light eternally entwine.
Oh, my love! Oh, my love!
You are the pulse that stirs the seas of my soul,
A tempest caught in the stillness of my heart,
Each word you speak, a tempest of wonder,
Each breath is a promise that binds us apart.
Oh, my love! Oh, my love!
Like a river running through the fabric of time,
You weave through my thoughts with delicate grace,
A tapestry of passion, both bitter and sweet,
A landscape I traverse, no end, no space.
Oh, my love! Oh, my love!
Can the heavens hold our eternal story,
Where shadows fade into the arms of light?
In the labyrinth of your eyes, I find my meaning,
A journey endless, in love's endless flight.